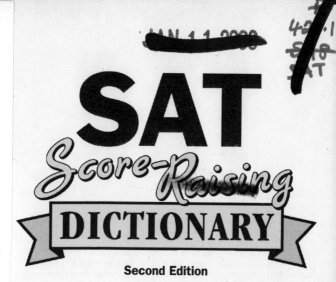

SAT

Score-Raising

DICTIONARY

Second Edition

A **Fun** and **Effective** Way to **Learn**

1,000

of the Most Frequently Tested

SAT WORDS

KAPLAN

PUBLISHING

New York

Editorial Director: Jennifer Farthing
Project Editor: Eric Titner
Cover Designer: Carly Schnur

Published by Kaplan Publishing, a division of Kaplan, Inc.
888 Seventh Ave.
New York, NY 10106

May 2007
10 9 8 7 6 5 4 3 2

ISBN-13: 978-1-4195-9711-4
ISBN-10:   1-4195-9711-6

For information about ordering Kaplan Publishing books at special quantity discounts, please call 1-800-KAP-ITEM or write to Kaplan Publishing, 888 Seventh Ave., 22nd floor, New York, NY 10106.

Hey, you!

Is it difficult to stay awake while memorizing those boring SAT vocabulary words? Do you find yourself wandering the bookstore hoping, JUST HOPING, to find something that will make learning SAT vocabulary words kind of . . . fun?

Yeah, we hear you—it's tough getting motivated to study, especially when there's so much other stuff going on in your busy life. That's why Kaplan came up with the *SAT Score-Raising Dictionary Second Edition*—to make memorizing vocabulary faster, easier . . . and maybe even fun, too!

So what makes Kaplan's *SAT Score-Raising Dictionary Second Edition* different from those other vocabulary prep books . . . you know, the BORING ones?

Lots of stuff! Kaplan offers you:

- a realistic number of SAT words to learn, as opposed to other books that overwhelm you with thousands of words you have little chance of memorizing with everything else you have to do this year

- parts of speech and pronunciations so you can incorporate the vocabulary words into everyday life (or at least impress your friends at parties)

- funny illustrations throughout to help you with word association and memorization

AND . . .

- The Kaplan *SAT Score-Raising Dictionary Second Edition* is the only book on the market that gives you fun sample sentences featuring high school students that you can identify with!

Read about the lives of ten students from Anytown High as you learn some of the most frequently tested words on the SAT. There's **Chantalle**, the popular girl everyone loves to hate and her best friend, **Shanna**, the overachieving class president; **Derek**, the mysterious rocker boy; **Willow**, the school's most notorious activist and vegetarian; **Josh**, the biggest jock in school; **George**, who was voted most likely to belch in public; the artist currently known as **Marisol**; **Timmy**, the neighborhood nerd; **Paul**, the jokester with a big heart; and **Ashley**, the peppiest cheerleader ever (yippee!).

So get on board with the kids of Anytown High and STOP PROCRASTINATING! Learning just a few words (and having a few laughs) will start you on your journey toward an awesome SAT score.

Good Luck!

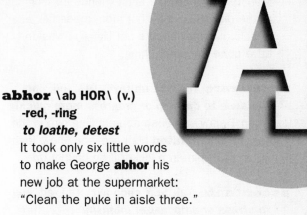

abhor \ab HOR\ (v.)
-red, -ring
to loathe, detest
It took only six little words
to make George **abhor** his
new job at the supermarket:
"Clean the puke in aisle three."

abrasive \ab RAY siv\ (adj.)
harsh and rough in manner
Ironically, the basketball coach's **abrasive** style
really motivated the team to win the game.

abridge \uh BRIJ\ (v.) -ed, -ing
to condense, shorten
Chantalle knew she had missed her curfew and
hoped her parents would give her the **abridged**
curfew lecture when she got home.

abrupt \ab RUP t\ (adj.)
sudden; curt
Shanna threw her arms around Paul when he
asked her to the prom but **abruptly** pulled back
when he announced that he was only kidding.

1

absolve \ab ZOLV\ (v.) -ed, -ing
to forgive, free from blame
Marisol **absolved** her artsy friends for laughing at the preppy sweater her mom made her wear to school—after all, it's not like she wouldn't have done the same thing.

accelerate \ak SEL uh rayt\ (v.) -ed, -ing
to cause to develop or progress more quickly
When Timmy saw Josh approaching him in the hall, he **accelerated** his pace—he knew Josh would stuff him in a locker if he caught up.

accentuate \ak SEN choo ayt\ (v.) -ed, -ing
to stress or emphasize; intensify
Despite what the fashion magazines said, Ashley was sure that the bright blue eye shadow **accentuated** her blue eyes perfectly.

accessible
\ak SESS ih bull\ (adj.)
attainable, available; approachable
Poor Shanna forgot to lock her journal, leaving her secrets **accessible** to her nosy little sister.

accomplice \ah KOMP liss\ (n.)
an associate in wrongdoing
Paul had no **accomplice** when he egged the principal's car—he did it all by himself.

accord \uh KORD\ (v.) -ed, -ing
to bestow upon
The bully told Timmy to give up his lunch money or he'd **accord** him a supersonic wedgie.

acquire \ah KWIYR\ (v.) -ed, -ing
to gain possession of
George **acquired** a taste for refried beans, much to the dismay of his classmates.

acrimony \AK ri MOW nee\ (n.)
bitterness, animosity
The homecoming game ended in **acrimony** after a few of the visiting team members started name-calling on the field.

adept \uh DEPT\ (adj.)
very skilled
It wasn't long before George became **adept** at "looking busy" when his boss needed someone to run an errand.

adorn \uh DORN\ (v.) -ed, -ing
to enhance or decorate
Derek **adorned** the walls of his room with posters of hot girls in bikinis, despite his mother's objections.

adulation \AJ e LAY shin\ (n.)
excessive flattery
Ashley, the cheerleading captain, enjoyed the **adulation** of the girls who wanted to make the squad.

advantageous \ADD van TAYJ ish\ (adj.)
favorable, useful
Chantalle found her reasoning skills **advantageous** when convincing her parents to let her go to Mexico for spring break.

adversary \ADD ver SEH ree\ (n.)
opponent, enemy
Shanna crushed her **adversary** in the race for class president and won the election by a landslide.

adversity \add VER si tee\ (n.)
a state of hardship or misfortune
One might say Ashley overcame **adversity** to become head cheerleader despite her lack of flexibility or tumbling skills.

aerate \ayr AYT\ (v.) -ed, -ing
expose to air
Josh's mom asked him to **aerate** his smelly sneakers outside the house.

aesthetic \ess THET ik\ (adj.)
pertaining to beauty or art
Chantalle's mom tried to convince Chantalle that the brown paisley shirt she'd bought was **aesthetic**, but Chantalle thought the print was totally outdated.

affectation \ah feck TAY shun\ (n.)
pretension; false display
Telling your math teacher how awesome he is just to get a good grade is an **affectation**.

affiliation \uh FILL ee AY shun\ (n.)
an association with a group or organization
Timmy pretended to have an **affiliation** with the tough guys hanging out by the bleachers so that people would think he had cool friends.

agile \AH jel\ (adj.)
well-coordinated, nimble
Ashley picked the most **agile** gymnasts to be on the cheerleading squad.

agitate \AH ji tayt\
(v.) -ed, -ing
upset, disturb
Paul liked to **agitate** his French teacher by speaking English with a French accent.

alacrity \uh LACK ri tee\ (adj.)
cheerful willingness, eagerness; speed
Shanna's sister agreed with **alacrity** to cover for Shanna after curfew, because Shanna said she'd pay her twenty bucks to do so.

allegation \ah leh GAY shun\ (n.)
claim without proof
Ashley could not prove her **allegations** about
her science teacher and her English teacher
dating...she just had a feeling.

alleviate \uh LEE vee ayt\
(v.) -ed, -ing
to relieve, improve partially
Timmy could do nothing to
alleviate his embarrass-
ment when he realized his
pants zipper had been open
all day.

amalgamation \uh MAL ga MAY shun\ (n.)
consolidation of smaller parts
Marisol's fashion statement was an
amalgamation of pieces from different eras.

ambiguous \am BIG yoo us\ (n.)
uncertain; subject to multiple interpretations
Marisol's painting was so **ambiguous** that
none of her classmates could figure out what it
was supposed to be about.

ambivalent \am BIV uh lent\ (adj.)
uncertain; emotionally conflicted
Shanna is **ambivalent** about using student
funds to either buy some teen fiction for the
library or to throw a rockin' senior dance.

amiable \A mee uh bull\ (adj.)
friendly, pleasant, likable
The substitute teacher seemed **amiable** at
first...until he whipped out a pop quiz.

amicable \AM i ka bull\ (adj.)
friendly, agreeable
Despite the fact that Willow and Marisol were
dating the same guy, they tried to maintain an
amicable relationship while working after
school at the Dairy Queen.

amorphous \ah MOR fus\ (adj.)
having no definite form
Shanna decided that the baggy prom dress she
bought made her look like an **amorphous** blob,
so she returned it.

amplify \AM pleh fy\
(v.) -ied, -ing
increase, intensify
Derek **amplified** the
sound on his speakers
drastically whenever he
played his electric guitar.

anachronistic \uh NAK ru NISS tik\ (n.)
outdated
Chantalle was horrified when the hairstylist
gave her a puffy, **anachronistic** hairstyle from
the 1980s.

anarchist \AN ar kist\ (n.)
one who aims for the overthrow of government
Derek pretended to be an **anarchist** like his friends, but he really thought the student government was doing a great job.

anecdote \AN ik dote\ (n.)
short, usually funny account of an event
The clarinet players had a good laugh over their band-camp **anecdotes**.

anonymous
\uh NON uh muss\ (n.)
unknown
Chantalle found an **anonymous** love note on her locker and vowed to find out who had left it.

antagonist \an TAG uh nist\ (n.)
foe, adversary, opponent
Willow and Derek have been **antagonists** ever since fifth grade, when he cut off her ponytail.

anthology \an THOL uh jee\ (n.)
collection of literary works
George hid his **anthology** of Superman comics behind his biology textbook so his teacher wouldn't catch him reading them in class.

anthropocentrism
\an throw po SEN chrizm\ (n.)
interpreting reality entirely based on human values
Willow finds the **anthropocentric** attitudes of her classmates upsetting and plans to start a petition banning people from wearing leather shoes.

antidote \an ti DOTE\ (n.)
a remedy, an agent used to counteract
Timmy thinks that dating a popular girl will be the **antidote** to his geek status.

apathetic \ap uh THET ik\ (n.)
indifferent, unconcerned
Some guys act **apathetic** around a girl they like in order to seem cool.

appalling \uh PAW ling\ (n.)
causing dismay, frightful
Shanna found George's constant farting **appalling**.

appraise \uh PRAYZ\ (v.) -ed, -ing
evaluate, estimate the value
Timmy asked Chantalle to **appraise** his cool factor. She said on a scale of 1 to 10, he was a −4.

arable \AR uh bull\ (adj.)
suitable for cultivation
The soil Marisol mixed in science class was not **arable** because Paul had slipped in some plaster of Paris when she wasn't looking.

arbitration
\ar bih TRAY shun\ (n.)
settlement of a dispute by an outside party
Shanna wanted **arbitration** between the students and the administration over whether or not the students deserved five extra minutes of lunchtime each day.

archaic \ar KAY ik\ (adj.)
antiquated, from an earlier time; outdated
Marisol was humiliated when her father displayed his **archaic** dance moves from the 1970s in front of her friends.

archetypal \ark uh TY pul\ (n.)
an ideal example of a type
Josh is the **archetypal** jock, playing varsity football in the fall and basketball and baseball in the spring.

archive \AR kiyv\ (v.) -ed, -ing
to place into storage
At sixteen years old, Ashley finally decided it was time to **archive** her blankey in the attic, along with her collection of stuffed animals.

ardor \AR dur\ (n.)
great emotion or passion
Ashley's **ardor** for cheerleading was evident when she cheered with infectious enthusiasm—even after she fell on her butt.

arid \AR id\ (adj.)
extremely dry or deathly boring
Josh knew it was time to dump his girlfriend when he dozed off during yet another **arid** phone conversation.

ascetic \uh SET ik\ (adj.)
self-denying, abstinent, and austere
Timmy resigned himself to an **ascetic** lifestyle . . . until a girl in the chess club miraculously asked him out.

assertion \uh SIR shun\ (n.)
declaration, usually without proof
Derek thought that Chantalle's **assertion** about getting any guy she wanted was hard to believe.

assess \uh SESS\ (v.) -ed, -ing
to establish a value
The supermarket manager **assessed** George's job performance and refused to give him a raise.

assiduous
\uh SI joo iss\ (adj.)
diligent, persistent, hardworking
Timmy was so **assiduous** about looking good for his date that he applied zit cream five times a day until the big event.

assurance \uh SHOOR ans\ (n.)
guarantee, pledge
Chantalle gave her **assurance** to her parents that she would not have a wild party while they were out of town. Of course, she was lying.

astute \uh STOOT\ (adj.)
having good judgment
George believed that he was an **astute** driver, but his six speeding tickets proved otherwise.

asylum \uh SY lum\ (n.)
a place offering protection and safety
After a rough day at school, Ashley seeks **asylum** in her bedroom, curled up with a mug of hot chocolate and a copy of *Teen Cheerleader* magazine.

attain \uh TAYN\ (n.)
to accomplish, gain
Timmy had a fantastic dream about moving away and **attaining** popularity in a brand-new high school.

atypical \ay TIP ih kul\ (adj.)
unusual, irregular
Even though they are enemies, Willow thinks
Derek's **atypical** purple Mohawk is totally hot.

audacious \aw DAY shis\ (adj.)
bold, daring, fearless
Ashley thought asking out a guy was totally
audacious, but Shanna found it pretty easy.

augment \awg MENT\ (v.) -ed, -ing
to expand, extend
George wanted to **augment** his salary, but did
not want to work the extra hours.

auspicious \aw SPISH iss\ (adj.)
having favorable prospects, promising
Shanna thought that getting an A on her first test
was an **auspicious** start to the school year.

authoritarian \aw THAR ih TAYR ee on\ (adj.)
demanding absolute obedience to authority
George's **authoritarian** boss did not take
kindly to George's napping on the lawn furniture
display at work.

autonomous \aw TON uh muss\ (adj.)
separate, independent
Derek likes to think that his cool, rocker look
makes him **autonomous** amidst the average
dregs at school.

avant-garde
\AH vant GARD\ (adj.)
radically new or original
Marisol's **avant-garde** sculpture made with toothpicks and peanut butter was so ahead of its time that her art teacher didn't "get it" and gave her an F on the project.

avian \AY vee on\ (adj.)
of, or relating to, birds
Timmy emitted an **avian** squawk of pain as he tried to pull out the gum that someone had thrown in his hair.

awe \AW\ (n.)
reverence, respect, wonder
Derek watched in **awe** as his favorite rock star jumped from chord to chord on his six-string.

balk \BAWK\ (v.) -ed, -ing
to refuse, shirk; prevent
Willow chained herself to the
hundred-year-old tree in her backyard
when her parents threatened to cut it down to
make room for an in-ground pool, and **balked**
when they tried to cut her free.

banality \buh NAL ih tee\ (n.)
*something that is trite, commonplace,
or predictable*
The other kids on the pep squad complained
about the **banality** of Ashley's fund-raising idea
to hold a bake sale; they wanted something
more exciting.

bane \BAYN\ (n.)
cause of harm or ruin; source of annoyance
*Why, oh why, does Josh have to be the **bane** of
my existence?* Timmy wondered as the hulking
jock shoved him into yet another locker.

banish \BAN ish\ (v.) -ed, -ing
drive away, expel
Chantalle didn't like the way Shanna was dressing lately, so she **banished** Shanna from the cool group for three weeks.

bard \BARD\ (n.)
lyrical poet
Timmy's friends in the poetry club have called him the **bard** ever since he wrote an inspiring ode to beef jerky.

belated \bee LAY tid\ (adj.)
having been delayed, done too late
Willow's **belated** effort to save the snails was a bust—by the time she got to the French restaurant, the patrons had eaten all the escargot.

belligerent \be LIJ er ent\ (adj.)
hostile, inclined to fight
Contrary to popular belief, Derek doesn't have a **belligerent** bone in his body. He's a lover, not a fighter!

benefactor \BEN eh fak tur\ (n.)
someone who helps others financially
Chantalle didn't need to get an after-school job when she already had two **benefactors** at her disposal—her parents.

benevolent \bu NEV uh lint\ (adj.)
friendly and helpful
Even though he's a jokester at school, the ladies at the senior center where Paul volunteers say he's the most **benevolent** boy they know.

benign \bi NIYN\ (adj.)
gentle, harmless
George's science teacher looked **benign**, but George knew that she exhibited quite a temper when students were late to class.

bequeath \bi KWEETH\
(v.) -ed, -ing
pass on, hand down
Ashley gushed when last year's homecoming queen **bequeathed** to her a crown, saber, and red velvet cape.

berate \bee RAYT\ (v.) -ed, -ing
to scold harshly
Marisol **berated** her little brother for messing up her art project.

bereft \be REFT\ (adj.)
deprived of or lacking something
Even though the diet brownies were **bereft** of anything resembling chocolate, Ashley swore they were tasty.

17

betray \be TRAY\ (v.) -ed, -ing
to be false or disloyal to
Derek's band, Snakebite, felt **betrayed** when,
one afternoon, he jammed with the band Venom.

bewilder \be WILL der\ (v.) -ed, -ing
to confuse or puzzle
Marisol was **bewildered** by Derek's long
stare as she walked past him. Did she have
something stuck in her teeth?

biased \BY ust\ (adj.)
prejudiced
Chantalle could not deny that she was **biased**
against anyone who wore T-shirts with pictures
of cats on them.

bilk \BILK\ (v.) -ed, -ing
to defraud, swindle
George caught the lunch ladies eating handfuls of
French fries, thereby **bilking** the students out of
their fair share of potatoes.

blaze \BLAYZ\ (v.) -ed, -ing
shine brightly, flare up suddenly
Shanna's newly dyed hair was so red it looked
like a **blaze** of fire bobbing through the crowd.

blemish \BLEM ish\ (n.)
imperfection, flaw
Ashley couldn't stop staring at the one **blemish**
on her otherwise stellar report card—a big fat F
in chorus.

boast \BOWST\ (v.) -ed, -ing
speak with excessive pride
Josh **boasted** to his friends that he would probably get athletic scholarships from every college he applied to.

boon \BOON\ (n.)
blessing, something to be thankful for
The long weekend was a **boon** to the students after a tough week of tests.

bourgeois \boor ZWA\ (adj.)
middle class
A typical **bourgeois** teenager's weekend involves at least one trip to the mall.

braggart \BRAG ert\ (n.)
someone who boasts continuously
Shanna boasted about herself so much during her campaign for student body president that she came off as a **braggart**.

brandish \BRAN dish\ (v.) -ed, -ing
wave menacingly
Timmy tried to ward off Josh's taunting in the lunchroom by **brandishing** the only weapon he could find: a hot dog.

brutality \broo TAL ih tee\ (n.)
ruthless, cruel, and unrelenting acts
Willow was just trying to free the worker bees from the captivity of the farmer's honeycomb, but the **brutality** of their stings made it clear that they did not want to be saved.

buffer \BUFF uhr\ (n.)
something that separates two entities
George used his mashed potatoes as a **buffer** between the roast beef and lima beans on his lunch plate.

buffoonery \bu FOO ner ee\ (n.)
acting like a clown or fool
Paul knew his **buffoonery** got him a lot of laughs in class, but could it get him a date?

buttress \BUT riss\ (v.) -ed, -ing
to reinforce or support
Timmy was so nervous about going on a date that he spent three weeks **buttressing** his confidence by practicing conversations in the mirror.

bypass \BI pass\ (v.) -ed, -ing
avoid
Derek figured he could **bypass** an office job when he grew up by becoming a rock star.

cacophony
\ke KOF o nee\ (n.)
jarring, unpleasant noise
Derek thinks his guitar riffs are
an art form; his parents think they're a
cacophony.

cadence \KAYD ns\ (n.)
rhythmic flow; marching beat
The **cadence** of the music kept the marching
band in step as they circled the football field.

cajole \ka JOL\ (v.) -ed, -ing
flatter, coax, persuade
Since Ashley is the ultimate daddy's girl, she
can **cajole** her father into giving her anything.

calamity \ka LAM uh tee\ (n.)
disaster, catastrophe
Timmy's date was a total **calamity** when he
tripped and accidentally pushed the girl into the
lake at the park.

calculating \KAL q lay ting\ (adj.)
shrewd, crafty
Chantalle was so **calculating** that she developed a plan to convince her parents to let her go skiing in Aspen during Christmas break.

calumny \KAL um nee\ (n.)
false and malicious accusation, misrepresentation, slander
Derek vowed to find the person who spread a **calumny** about him lip-synching during the Battle of the Bands.

camaraderie
\kahm RAH da ree\ (n.)
trust, sociability amongst friends
Timmy likes the **camaraderie** of his friends in the accordion club.

cantankerous \kan TANK uh russ\ (adj.)
disagreeable, quarrelsome
George became **cantankerous** when his boss at the supermarket docked his pay for eating forty-two bags of chips on the job when he had only eaten forty-one.

carnivorous \kar NIV uh riss\ (adj.)
meat-eating
Willow believes that humans are not supposed to be **carnivorous** because their teeth are not very sharp.

carouse \kuh ROWZ\ (v.) -ed, -ing
to partake in drunken amusement, drink excessively
Paul promised his parents that when he turns twenty-one, he will not **carouse** in bars.

cartographer \kar TOG ruh fer\ (n.)
someone who makes maps
When George found out a **cartographer** was visiting his social studies class that day to give a lesson on maps, he decided to skip out and take an extra lunch period instead.

castigate \KASS ti gayt\ (v.) -ed, -ing
to punish, chastise, criticize severely
Marisol's mother **castigated** her for failing two subjects in school.

catalyst \KAT uh list\ (n.)
something causing change without being changed
Chantalle's new kitty was the **catalyst** that changed her opinion about people who wear shirts with cats on them—now she thought they were cool.

catastrophic \kat uh STROF ik\ (adj.)
of, or relating to, a terrible event or complete failure
In a **catastrophic** turn of events, Marisol left her art portfolio on the bus and had nothing to show the admissions counselors at F.I.T.

caustic \KAW stik\ (adj.)
biting, sarcastic; able to burn
Timmy brushed off Josh's **caustic** comments about his being in the poetry club. Timmy knew Josh was just jealous because he got a 56 on his last English test and Timmy got 100.

censor \SEN sur\ (v.) -ed, -ing
to examine and suppress information
Willow started a petition to stop the principal from **censoring** controversial books that were in the school library.

censure \SEN sher\ (v.) -ed, -ing
to find fault with and condemn as wrong; blame
Madame La Bouche **censured** Derek in front of the class for not doing his French homework.

cerebral \suh REE brell\ (adj.)
intellectual
Shanna was looking to date a **cerebral** type who enjoyed conversations about classic literature just as much as she did.

challenge \CHAL enj\ (v.) -ed, -ing
take exception to, call into question
George liked to **challenge** the authority of his boss by goofing off and seeing how much he could get away with.

chapped \CHAP t\ (adj.)
rough, cracked, or reddened by cold or exposure
Chantalle's **chapped** hands were a direct result of being too cool to wear gloves during the harsh winter.

cherish \CHER ish\ (v.) -ed, -ing
to remember fondly, treat with affection
Chantalle gave her boyfriend the line about **cherishing** the good times they'd had together—right before she dumped him.

circuitous \sir Q ih tuss\ (adj.)
indirect, taking the longest route
When Ashley goes jogging after school, she takes a **circuitous** route with lots of twists and turns so she doesn't get bored.

circumlocution \SIR kuhm low Q shin\ (n.)
roundabout, lengthy way of saying something
The gym teacher did not appreciate George's endless **circumlocution** about how he would never, ever wear a Speedo.

circumscribe \sir kum SKRIYB\ (v.) -ed, -ing
to encircle; set limits on, confine
Josh's ability to make jump shots was **circumscribed** by his short height.

civility \sih VILL ih tee\ (n.)
courtesy, politeness
Girls like going out on dates with Paul because he treats them with the utmost **civility**.

clairvoyant \klayr VOY nt\ (adj.)
exceptionally insightful, able to foresee the future
Willow was pumped when the **clairvoyant** psychic told her she was going to meet a hot guy at the Earth Day festival.

clamp \KLAMP\ (v.) -ed, -ing
establish by authority, impose
The principal vowed to **clamp** down on the kids who kept putting "kick me" signs on his back— just as soon as he figured out who they were.

clandestine \klan DES tin\ (adj.)
secretive, concealed for a darker purpose
Lisa paid a **clandestine** visit to her sister Shanna's room every day so she could read Shanna's diary.

clarity \KLAR it ee\ (n.)
clearness; clear understanding
Shanna told Timmy with the utmost **clarity** that she would not go out with him.

cliché \klee SHAY\ (n.)
overused expression or idea
Derek thought his latest rock song, *When Life Gives You Lemons, Make Lemonade*, was totally original, but really it was one big **cliché**.

clientele \kly en TELL\ (n.)
body of customers or patrons
George thought the **clientele** at the supermarket where he worked was kind of smelly.

clique \KLIK\ (n.)
small exclusive group
Chantalle was the leader of the popular **clique** at school.

cloying \KLOY ing\ (adj.)
overly sweet to the point of distaste or disgust
Chantalle wanted to barf as the **cloying** words came out of her mouth, but she really needed to butter up her math teacher in order to get a good grade.

cognizant \KOG ni zent\ (adj.)
fully informed, conscious
Josh was **cognizant** of the three girls who had crushes on him and winked at each one as they passed by.

coherent \ko HEE rent\ (adj.)
intelligible, lucid, understandable
George wasn't fully **coherent** until third period because he had gone to bed really late the night before.

cohesion \ko HEE zhun\ (n.)
act or state of sticking together; close union
Derek's band achieved the perfect **cohesion** of music and lyrics as they played a seamless concert.

collaborator \kuh LAB uh RAY tor\ (n.)
someone who helps on a task
Willow's **collaborator** at the animal shelter was a cute boy who held the puppies while she clipped their nails.

collage \ko LAZH\ (n.)
assemblage of diverse elements
Marisol's latest project was a **collage** of fashion magazine covers she called Face Á La Mode.

colloquial \ka LOW kwee ul\ (adj.)
characteristic of informal speech
Paul used a **colloquial** style of speech when hanging out with friends, but he spoke formally when he was with adults.

collusion \ku LOO zhen\ (n.)
collaboration, conspiracy
The principal found out that Josh, in **collusion** with Paul, put the whoopee cushion on his chair.

colossal \kuh LOS ul\ (n.)
immense, enormous
Chantalle and Shanna realized they made a
colossal error by not shopping together for
dresses to wear to the school dance; they
wound up wearing the same one.

combative \kom BAT iv\ (adj.)
eager to fight
Willow was not usually **combative**, but she
couldn't help arguing with a woman on the
street who was wearing a fur coat.

combustion
\kom BUS chen\ (n.)
the process of burning
Timmy studied the
combustion of the
marshmallow as he held it
over the Boy Scout campfire.

commemorate \kuh MEM uh rayt\ (v.) -ed, -ing
to serve as a memorial to
Shanna bought a pair of earrings every April
22nd to **commemorate** the day she got her
ears pierced.

commentary \KOM un teh ree\ (n.)
series of explanations or interpretations
Chantalle's mother told Chantalle to stop gossiping
about her classmates; Chantalle said she was
merely giving her **commentary** on the day's events.

comparable \KOM pur uh bul\ (adj.)
similar or equivalent
Derek liked to think that his band's style was
comparable to none, but there were tons of
rival groups with the same sound.

compassion \kum PASH in\ (n.)
sympathy, helpfulness, or mercy
Willow's **compassion** led her
to take an injured bird to the
animal shelter.

compelling
\kom PELL ing\ (adj.)
*urgently requiring atten-
tion, forceful*
Shanna is head of the debate team because
she always delivers a **compelling**
argument that drives home the team's objective.

compensate \KOMP en sayt\ (v.) -ed, -ing
to repay or reimburse
Timmy was **compensated** with a kiss on the
cheek from Ashley for tutoring her in math.

complacence \kom PLAY senss\ (n.)
self-satisfaction, lack of concern
George's **complacence** about studying quickly
ended when he realized he was in danger of
failing a class.

complement \KOMP leh ment\ (v.) -ed, -ing
to complete, perfect
The fuzzy black tail **complemented** the cat costume Chantalle would wear to the Halloween party.

complex \kom PLEKS\ (adj.)
intricate, complicated
Ashley's dance routine for the school talent show was so **complex** that she accidentally fell off the stage while performing it.

compliant \kom PLY int\ (adj.)
submissive and yielding
Chantalle likes having **compliant** friends so that she can get them to do things for her.

composed \kom POSD\ (adj.)
serene, calm
After Willow took a few cleansing breaths, she felt **composed** enough to begin her presentation to her science class on the dangers of genetically engineered fruit.

comprehensible \kom pree HEN sih bul\ (adj.)
readily understood
George thought that calculus was too complicated to be **comprehensible** without a tutor.

comprehensive \kom pree HEN siv\ (adj.)
very large in scope
Derek has a **comprehensive** knowledge of
music, both popular and obscure.

compulsion
\kom PUL shin\ (n.)
*an irresistible impulse
to act*
Ashley tried to stop her
compulsion to bite her
fingernails by polishing her
nails with sour-tasting polish.

compute \kom PYOOT\ (v.) -ed, -ing
to determine by mathematics
It's odd how Chantalle is failing math, yet she
can **compute** 30 percent off a sale item without a calculator.

conceited \kon SEET id\ (adj.)
holding an unduly high opinion of oneself, vain
Even Chantalle agreed it was a little **conceited**
to check out her reflection in the silverware.

conceivable \kon SEEV uh bull\ (adj.)
capable of being understood
It's **conceivable** that Timmy will go to college
after he graduates high school because he is
the smartest boy in his class.

conciliatory \kon SILL ee uh tory\ (adj.)
overcoming distrust or hostility
Timmy gave Josh a **conciliatory** handshake
after Josh apologized for shoving Timmy's head
in the toilet.

concoct \kon KOKT\ (v.) -ed, -ing
to devise, using skill and intelligence
George knew he would have to **concoct** a good
reason for skipping social studies class or he
would be in big trouble.

concordant \kon KOR dint\ (adj.)
harmonious, agreeing
The geometry class was **concordant** on the fact
that their teacher gave them too much homework.

condemnation \kon dem NAY shun\ (n.)
*an expression of strong
disapproval*
Shanna's **condemnation**
of four-inch platforms
was brought on when
she twisted her ankle
while wearing a pair.

condense \kon DENS\
(v.) -ed, -ing
to reduce, make more concise
Marisol **condensed** her art portfolio to twenty
of her strongest pieces.

condescending \con di SEN ding\ (adj.)
possessing an attitude of superiority,
patronizing
The seniors are always **condescending** to the
freshmen because the seniors have been there
a lot longer and think they know more than the
freshmen do.

condolence \kon DOH lens\ (n.)
sympathy for a person's misfortune
Shanna offered her **condolences** to Chantalle
when Chantalle broke a fingernail.

condone \kon DOHN\ (v.) -ed, -ing
to pardon or forgive; overlook,
justify, or excuse a fault
The principal did not **condone**
speaking in homeroom during
morning announcements.

conduit \KON doo it\ (n.)
tube, pipe, or similar passage
The girls' bathroom was Ashley's **conduit** to gossip about the boys—she could hear them through
the air vents, talking in the boys' bathroom.

configuration \kon fig yu RAY shun\ (n.)
arrangement of parts or elements
Each day Chantalle dictates the seating
configuration at her lunch table. Next it would
be boy, girl, boy, girl.

confiscation \kon fis KAY shun\ (n.)
seizure by authorities
The **confiscation** of Derek's iPod in class made him so angry he kicked his locker on the way to his next class.

conflict \KON flikt\ (n.)
a clash, a battle
Josh couldn't remember how his **conflict** with Timmy began, but he continued to torture him anyway.

conformity \kon FORM ih tee\ (n.)
similarity in form or character
Marisol is totally against **conformity**. Her clothing style is nothing like that of any of the other kids at school.

confound \kun FOWND\
(v.) -ed, -ing
to baffle, perplex
Josh, **confounded** by the complicated football play, threw a pass that was intercepted by the opposing team.

confrontational \kon fron TAY shun al\ (adj.)
eager to come face-to-face with in an adversarial manner
Timmy was not a **confrontational** kind of guy, but he knew that he would have to stand up to his bully, Josh, sooner or later.

congeal \kun JEEL\
(v.) -ed, -ing
*to become thick or solid,
as a liquid freezing*
Marisol watched the gravy **congeal** on her mashed potatoes and decided to head back to the lunch line to grab a PB&J sandwich.

consecrate \KON si krayt\ (v.) -ed, -ing
to declare sacred; dedicate to a goal
Josh **consecrated** his purple underwear and wore them at every home football game—whether they were clean or not.

consensus \kon SEN suss\ (n.)
unanimity, agreement of opinion or attitude
After much debate, Shanna and the rest of the student council reached a **consensus** and decided to have a car wash as a senior-trip fundraiser.

conservatism \kon SUR va tizm\ (n.)
inclination to maintain traditional values
Marisol knew her new nose ring was going to clash with her parents' **conservatism**.

conserve \kon SERV\ (v.) -ed, -ing
use sparingly; protect from loss or harm
Willow decided to take a shower only once a week to **conserve** water.

consolation \kon so LAY shun\ (n.)
something providing comfort or solace for a loss or hardship
The twenty bucks Timmy found on the floor was a small **consolation** for tripping and splitting his pants in front of a large crowd.

constellation \kon stuh LAY shun\ (n.)
a collection of stars with a perceived design
When her date told her she was as beautiful as the **constellation** Orion, Ashley realized he was a little too corny for her to go out with again.

consummate \KON suh mit\ (adj.)
accomplished, complete, perfect
Shanna delivered the **consummate** debate speech, so perfect it even convinced her opponent to change his position.

consumption \kon SUMP shun\ (n.)
the act of eating or taking in
Ashley's **consumption** of five cans of soda before bed kept her awake all night.

contagious
\kon TAY jus\ (adj.)
spreading from one to another
The supermarket manager said that George's laziness was **contagious** and was spreading to the rest of the employees.

contaminate \kon TAM uh nayt\ (v.) -ed, -ing
to make impure by contact
Despite his parents' warning that television **contaminates** the mind, George had no problem watching 20 hours of TV every weekend.

contemplate \KON tem playt\ (v.) -ed, -ing
to consider carefully
Timmy had to seriously **contemplate** where he wanted to apply to college.

contemporary \kon TEMP uh rery\ (adj.)
belonging to the same period of time
Chantalle vowed to get Marisol to wear **contemporary** clothes one day instead of the vintage styles she always had on.

contemptuous \kon TEMP shoo us\ (adj.)
scornful, disdainful
Willow shot Derek a **contemptuous** look when he played his new song, *Willow's a Loser*, in the lunchroom.

content \kon TENT\ (adj.)
satisfied
Josh is **content** to be known in school as a jock. After all, he does play three varsity sports.

contract \kon TRAKT\ (v.) -ed, -ing
acquire, incur
Willow thinks she **contracted** a cold waiting in the rain for the bus.

contradiction \kon tra DIK shun\ (n.)
statement opposite to what was already said
Timmy corrected the teacher when he noticed
what she said was a **contradiction** to what
was in the textbook.

contrite \kon TRYT\ (adj.)
deeply sorrowful and repentant for a wrong
Shanna felt **contrite** for making fun of Timmy
after she saw the sad expression on his face.

conundrum \ka NUN drum\ (n.)
riddle, puzzle, or problem with no solution
Josh found himself with a
conundrum when he realized
that his upcoming baseball
game overlapped with his
basketball game—how
would he play at both?

convention \kon VEN shen\ (n.)
general acceptance of practices or attitudes
Shanna followed the **convention** of a typical
overachiever. She excelled in all her classes
and joined as many extracurricular activities as
humanly possible.

conventional \kon VEN sheh nell\ (adj.)
typical, customary, commonplace
Conventional fast-food restaurants have a drive-
thru window so their customers can order and
pick up their food without getting out of their cars.

convergence \kun VER jinss\ (n.)
the state of separate elements joining or coming together
A **convergence** of rumors led Ashley to believe that her crush was about to ask her to the prom.

convey \kon VAY\ (v.) -ed, -ing
to transport; to make known
Unfortunately, George **conveyed** his appreciation for pretty girls by making kissing noises at them.

convict \kon VICT\ (v.) -ed, -ing
to find guilty of a crime
Madame La Bouche, the French teacher, **convicted** Paul of shooting the spitball when she found him hiding a straw under his desk.

conviction \kon VIC shin\ (n.)
fixed or strong belief
Shanna spoke with **conviction** when she addressed the student body—it was one of the things that made her a good class president.

convoluted \KON vuh loo tid\ (adj.)
twisted, complicated, involved
Paul loved English, but he thought calculus theories were too **convoluted** to make any sense.

cordial \KOR jel\ (adj.)
warm and sincere, friendly
Chantalle offered Derek a **cordial** smile in the hallway even though the two rarely spoke to each other.

corrective \koh REK tiv\ (adj.)
intended to fix, remedy
Marisol hardly wore her **corrective** glasses
even though she could barely see without them.

corroborate \ke ROB uh rayt\ (v.) -ed, -ing
to confirm, verify
Paul's information **corroborated** Shanna's fear
that the student council wanted to impeach her.

corrosive
\ku ROW siv\ (adj.)
*gradually destructive,
steadily harmful*
The dentist told
George that soda was
corrosive to his teeth,
but that didn't stop George
from drinking it.

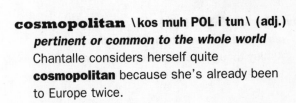

cosmopolitan \kos muh POL i tun\ (adj.)
pertinent or common to the whole world
Chantalle considers herself quite
cosmopolitan because she's already been
to Europe twice.

counteract \kown ter ACT\ (v.) -ed, -ing
to oppose the effects by contrary action
Ashley started spreading rumors about Shanna
to **counteract** the rumors Shanna was telling
about her.

crafty \KRAF tee\ (adj.)
underhanded, devious, or deceptive
Timmy devised a **crafty** plan to give Josh at least one supersonic wedgie before graduation.

crass \KRASS\ (adj.)
crude, unrefined
George couldn't believe that Shanna had called him **crass**; he belched only once during lunch.

credo \KREE doh\ (n.)
system of principles or beliefs
Paul's **credo** is "Do unto others as you would have them do unto you."

crescendo \kruh SHEN do\ (n.)
gradual increase in volume, force, or intensity
The band ended their final song of the night with a huge **crescendo**.

crude \KROOD\ (adj.)
unrefined, natural; blunt, offensive
Ashley thought Josh's remark about their teacher's hairy legs was totally **crude**.

cue \Q\ (n.)
reminder, prompt
Marisol shone the spotlight on Derek, center stage, giving him the **cue** to sing.

culpable \KUL puh bull\ (adj.)
guilty, responsible for wrong
Willow knew George was **culpable** for eating her brownie thanks to the incriminating chocolate smudges around his mouth.

cumulative \KYOOM yuh lah tiv\ (adj.)
resulting from gradual increase
Paul's inability to sleep was the **cumulative** effect of his drinking six cups of coffee that day.

cunning \KUN ing\ (adj.)
given to artful deception
Chantalle, as **cunning** as she is beautiful, thinks she would make the perfect spy.

curator \q RAY ter\ (n.)
caretaker and overseer of an exhibition, especially in a museum
The **curator** of the museum yelled at Marisol to stop touching the famous painting.

curtail \ker TAYL\ (v.) -ed, -ing
to shorten
Willow **curtailed** the time she spent on her date because the guy kept talking about how he thought vegetarians were narrow-minded.

dangle \DANG gul\
(v.) -ed, -ing
to hang loosely and swing
George laughed as he **dangled**
a piece of candy in front of a baby,
then pulled it away, making the baby cry.

dated \DAY tid\ (adj.)
old-fashioned, out of style
Shanna wore her mother's neon-pink sweatshirt
and a pair of matching leg warmers over her
jeans; the look was totally **dated** but perfect for
a Halloween costume.

daunting \DAWN ting\ (adj.)
discouraging
Living in a tree for three weeks might be a
daunting task for some, but Willow was
determined to do it to become one with nature.

debacle \di BAK ul\ (n.)
disastrous collapse, total failure
The DJ at the dance was so bad that everyone left
early, making the evening a complete **debacle**.

debase \de BAYS\ (v.) -ed, -ing
to degrade or lower in quality or stature
Paul **debased** the statue of the school's founder by hanging a pair of underwear from the statue's head.

debilitating \dee BIL uh tay ting\ (adj.)
impairing the strength or energy of
Timmy's fear of public speaking was so **debilitating** that he couldn't even practice in front of his goldfish.

debtor \DET ur\ (n.)
someone that owes something to someone else
Shanna is Chantalle's **debtor** because Shanna *so* owes Chantalle for getting her a date with the cute foreign-exchange student.

debunk \dee BUNK\ (v.) -ed, -ing
to expose the falseness of
Willow convinced her parents to get a dog and a cat so that she can **debunk** the theory that dogs and cats can't live together.

deceive \de SEEV\ (v.) -ed, -ing
mislead, give false impression
Chantalle has **deceived** her classmates into thinking that she's a tough cookie, but in reality she is very sensitive.

decibel \DEH sib ul\ (n.)
unit of sound intensity
Derek's mom told him to turn down the **decibel**
level on his amplifier because the neighbors
were complaining about the noise.

decisive \de SIY siv\ (adj.)
conclusive; capable of determining outcome
Grades, extracurricular activities, and an SAT score
are **decisive** factors in college admissions.

decorous \de KOHR us\ (adj.)
proper, well-behaved
The ladies at the senior citizen's center often
remarked on Paul's refreshing **decorous**
behavior, which they thought was unlike that of
most of today's teens.

deduction \dee DUK shin\ (n.)
the drawing of a conclusion through logic
It was simple **deduction** that led Shanna to the
conclusion that her sister, Lisa, was reading her
journal. Lisa had left her Snoopy bookmark in
between the pages.

defective
\dee FEK tiv\ (adj.)
faulty
Shanna realized that her
new compact was **defec-
tive** when she opened it and
noticed the mirror was cracked.

deferment \de FUR ment\ (n.)
the act of delaying
Chantalle asked her parents for a **deferment** from being grounded because of a hot party she wanted to attend that weekend. They said, "No."

defiantly \de FI ant lee\ (adv.)
boldly resisting
Marisol **defiantly** told her parents that she would not apply to any four-year college that wasn't an art school even though they wanted her to.

deficit \DEF ih sit\ (n.)
inadequacy, disadvantage
Timmy is at a bit of a **deficit** when it comes to social skills.

deft \DEFT\ (adj.)
skillful, dexterous
Josh **deftly** dodged his opponent, then slam-dunked the basketball, winning the game for his team.

degradation \deh gruh DAY shun\ (n.)
reduction in worth or dignity
Shanna was fired as editor in chief of the yearbook, but she hid her **degradation** by saying that she had resigned from the job.

delegate \DEL uh gayt\ (v.) -ed, -ing
to give powers to another
Chantalle planned to have a party at her house, but she **delegated** all of the setup to her friends.

deleterious
\de le TEER ee us\ (adj.)
harmful, destructive, detrimental
Willow stayed awake all night worrying about **deleterious** fuel emissions from cars that were destroying the ozone layer.

deliberation \de lib uh RAY shun\ (n.)
discussion or careful consideration of an issue
After much **deliberation**, Josh's parents agreed to let him use the car on Saturday.

delineate \de LIN ee ayt\ (v.) -ed, -ing
to portray, depict, describe
Shanna **delineated** to her parents her plan to become president of the United States one day.

demagogue \DEM uh gog\ (n.)
leader, rabble-rouser, usually appealing to emotion or prejudice
Fighting broke out at a school pep rally when one boy acted like a **demagogue** and said hateful things about a rival school.

demean \di MEEN\ (v.) -ed, -ing
to degrade, humiliate, humble
Derek believes that singing
cover songs would
demean the "street
cred" of his band.

demeanor
\de MEE ner\ (n.)
the way a person behaves
Some say Willow has a calming
demeanor; others say she's just boring.

demolish \de MOL ish\ (v.) -ed, -ing
destroy, damage severely
Josh roused his teammates by saying that they
were going to **demolish** the other team and win
the basketball game by sixty points.

demolition \de muh LISH un\ (n.)
the act of destroying
Timmy didn't believe that the **demolition**
of his science project was an accident;
he suspected sabotage.

demonize \DEE mun iyz\ (v.) -ed, -ing
to represent as evil
George **demonized** his former first-grade
teacher, telling his little sister that the
teacher ate children who didn't behave
in the classroom.

depose \dee POZ\ (v.) -ed, -ing
*to remove from a high position,
as from a throne*
Derek couldn't believe that the other members
of his band, Snakebite, **deposed** him as lead
singer just because he had jammed with
another band.

derelict \DER uh likt\ (adj.)
neglectful of one's obligations; abandoned
It's true that George was being **derelict** in his job
duties at the supermarket. It is also true that he
scored a cute girl's number instead of working.

deride \di RIYD\ (v.) -ed, -ing
to mock, ridicule, make fun of
Josh **derided** Timmy for wearing a "Nerds
Rule!" T-shirt.

derivative \di RIV uh tiv\ (adj.)
copied or adapted; not original
Chantalle and Shanna both had on an outfit
derivative of what the other had
worn the day before. Who
was copying whom?

desolate
\DES uh lit\ (adj.)
deserted, lifeless, barren
The school was **desolate**
after all the students had left
for the weekend.

despotism \DES puh tizm\ (n.)
dominance through threat of violence
Some might say that Josh's **despotism** occurs not because he's a tough guy, but because he is insecure.

destitution \des tih TOO shun\ (n.)
complete poverty
If Willow could have only one wish granted it would be to abolish **destitution** so that everyone in the world would have food, shelter, and cable television.

determine \di TUR min\ (v.) -ed, -ing
to decide, establish
Ashley was unable to **determine** what she should wear to the party, so she called Shanna for advice.

detractor \di TRAK tur\ (n.)
someone who belittles something else
Chantalle's **detractors** noted that although she is pretty and popular, she probably isn't all that smart.

devious \DEE vee us\ (adj.)
shifty, not straightforward
Ashley felt a little **devious** as she snuck into the kitchen and ate the last cupcake, which her brother had reserved for himself.

devour \di VOWR\ (v.) -ed, -ing
eat greedily, consume
Paul stared, amazed, as George **devoured** his entire bowl of spaghetti in one gulp.

disclose \dis CLOZ\ (v.) -ed, -ing
to make known, expose
Marisol refused to **disclose** the identity of the cute boy who was hugging her in the photo.

didactic \di DAK tik\ (adj.)
excessively instructive
Ashley doesn't like **didactic** lectures from her parents; she prefers to learn life lessons by making her own mistakes.

diffident \DIF ih dint\ (adj.)
shy, lacking confidence
Something about the pretty new girl in school made Josh feel so **diffident**, he couldn't say a word to her.

diffuse \di FYOOS\ (adj.)
widely spread out
Willow wanted to barf from the **diffused** odor of cheap perfume in the girls' bathroom.

dignity \DIG nih tee\ (n.)
poise and self-respect
Shanna conducted herself with **dignity** when her date canceled on her at the last minute, even though she really wanted to give him a piece of her mind.

digression \di GRESH un\ (n.)
the act of straying; an instance of straying
Ashley found it difficult to work with her classmate on the history project because every time she mentioned World War I he would go into a **digression** about his parents' divorce.

dilatory \DIL uh tor ee\ (adj.)
slow, tending to delay
Chantalle gave a **dilatory** response to Josh's invitation to hang out on Saturday, just in case something better came along in the meantime.

diminish \di MIN ish\ (v.) -ed, -ing
to make smaller
No matter how much zit cream Timmy used, he was not able to **diminish** the bulbous pimple on his nose.

dingy \DIN gee\ (adj.)
shabby, drab
Chantalle thought that her nail polish was looking a little **dingy**, so she got a manicure.

disavow \dis uh VOW\
(v.) -ed, -ing
to refuse to acknowledge
Ashley **disavowed** any knowledge of her surprise birthday party, even though she arrived wearing a brand-new party dress.

discern \di SURN\ (v.) -ed, -ing
to perceive something obscure
George wondered if his boss could **discern** that
he was lying about why he was late for work.

discomfit \dis KUM fit\ (v.) -ed, -ing
make uneasy, embarrass
Marisol told her parents to "get a room" when
she was **discomfited** by their gross display of
affection at the breakfast table.

disconcert
\dis kuhn SURT\ (v.) -ed, -ing
*ruffle, upset one's self-
possession*
The coach was **discon-
certed** when the star
player of the football team
remarked that he would not
have time to play next year.

discord \DIS kord\ (n.)
lack of agreement; inharmonious combination
The **discord** between best friends Chantalle
and Shanna was evident when they didn't sit
together during lunch.

discourse \DIS kors\ (n.)
verbal exchange, conversation
Timmy wanted to settle his argument with Josh
through **discourse**, but Josh shoved him into a
locker instead.

discourteous \dis KUR tee us\ (adj.)
rude
Paul bumped into a girl at the mall and quickly apologized, not wanting to seem **discourteous**.

discredit \diss KRED it\ (v.) -ed, -ing
to harm the reputation of; dishonor or disgrace
Willow hoped to **discredit** the popular tanning salon by revealing to its customers that tanning beds are harmful to one's skin.

discrepancy \dis KREP un see\ (n.)
difference between
George was outraged to find a **discrepancy** between the number of hours he worked and the number of hours he was paid for. His boss explained that although George showed up for ten hours, he actually only worked for three.

discretion \dis KRESH in\ (n.)
ability to judge on one's own
Marisol's mom said Marisol could decorate her room at her own **discretion**, hence, why each wall was painted a different color.

discretionary
\dis KRESH uh ner ee\ (adj.)
subject to one's own judgment
As student body president, one might think that Shanna has **discretionary** power, but she has to get all of her ideas approved by the principal.

disdain \diss DAYN\ (v.) -ed, -ing
to regard with scorn or contempt
Josh **disdained** the other dodgeball players in the gym because he knew that he was undeniably the greatest dodgeballer of them all.

disheveled \di SHEV uld\ (adj.)
marked by disorder, untidy
Shanna neatened her hair between classes because she didn't like to look **disheveled**.

disingenuous \dis in JEN yoo us\ (adj.)
not straightforward, insincere
Timmy had a feeling that Josh was being **disingenuous** when he said he'd never give Timmy another wedgie.

disinterested \dis IN tur est id\ (adj.)
indifferent
George's **disinterested** attitude toward economics was clear when he fell asleep in class.

dismissal \dis MIS ul\ (n.)
act of being fired or let out
The seniors were psyched about their early **dismissal** from school.

disparage \di SPAR ij\ (v.) -ed, -ing
to belittle, speak disrespectfully about
Shanna thought that **disparaging** her sister's awful singing skills would make her sister stop singing around the house, but it didn't.

disparate \dis PAR it\ (adj.)
dissimilar, different in kind
Marisol broke up with her boyfriend because they had **disparate** personalities; she had a sense of humor and he didn't.

dispel \dis PELL\ (v.) -ed, -ing
to drive out or scatter
George's rocking SAT score **dispelled** any remarks about him being stupid.

display \dis PLAY\ (v.) -ed, -ing
to show, to exhibit, to present
Marisol was psyched to get a chance to **display** her artwork in the school's auditorium.

disputant \dis PYOO tent\ (n.)
someone in an argument
Paul is rarely a **disputant**, since he's a cheerful, outgoing guy.

disregard \dis rih GARD\ (v.) -ed, -ing
ignore
Shanna told the driving instructor that she did not **disregard** the stop sign; she just didn't see it.

dissemble \dih SEM bul\ (v.) -ed, -ing
to pretend, disguise one's motives
George **dissembled** just a bit when he told the college admissions officer that he was hard-working and conscientious.

disseminate \dih SEM uh nayt\ (v.) -ed, -ing
  to spread far and wide
  Willow **disseminated** her "Give Peace A Chance"
  e-mail to all 3,458 people on her buddy list.

dissipate \DIS uh payt\ (v.) -ed, -ing
  to vanish; to pursue pleasure to excess
  The stench from George's flatulence gradually
  dissipated, allowing people to come back into
  the room.

distant \DIS tent\ (adj.)
  separate, far apart
  Last summer, Chantalle visited
  her **distant** relatives in France.

distinctive
\dis TINK tiv\ (adj.)
  distinguishing characteristic
Paul's piercing blue eyes are his most
distinctive feature.

distortion \dis TOR shun\ (n.)
  misrepresentation; the act of twisting out of shape
  Shanna told Chantalle that her ugly haircut
  looked awesome, which was a major **distortion**
  of the truth.

distract \dis TRAKT\ (v.) -ed, -ing
  to cause to lose focus, to divert attention
  Timmy tried studying in a coffee shop, but the
  noise **distracted** him and he couldn't concentrate.

divert \di VURT\ (v.) -ed, -ing
to turn aside, to distract
Shanna slipped unseen into her bedroom after curfew, while her sister **diverted** her mom's attention.

divination \div uh NAY shin\ (n.)
foretelling the future using supernatural means
Marisol thought it would be fun to use **divination** to predict whether or not she'd get a date for the dance, so she pulled out her Ouija board.

divisive \dih VIY siv\ (adj.)
creating disunity or conflict
The notion of school uniforms caused a **divisive** rift between the kids who thought fashion was a creative outlet and others who believed it was a distraction from learning.

divulge \di VULJ\ (v.) -ed, -ing
to make known
Paul was embarrassed when Marisol walked by just as he was **divulging** to his friend his secret crush on her.

dogmatic \dog MAT ik\ (adj.)
rigidly fixed in opinion, opinionated
Willow couldn't help taking a **dogmatic** stand on issues because when she believed in something, she believed in it all the way.

dominant \DOM uh nent\ (adj.)
most prominent, exercising the most control
The **dominant** reason for the track star winning the 100-meter dash was not her talent, but her extreme competitiveness.

drab \JRAB\ (adj.)
faded, dull, dreary
Marisol thought her living room walls were a bit **drab**, so she painted them bright pink—a gesture her parents did not appreciate.

drawback \JRAW back\ (n.)
disadvantage, inconvenience
Timmy thought the fact that he was really scrawny was another **drawback** he didn't want to deal with, so he decided to start working out.

drought \JROWT\ (n.)
long period of abnormally low rainfall
Willow saved her sunflowers from the **drought** by watering them three times a day.

drub \JRUB\ (v.) -bed, -bing
defeat soundly, beat
The crowd went crazy as Josh stole the football and made a touchdown, **drubbing** the visiting team in the last minutes of the game.

dual \DOO ul\ (adj.)
having two parts, double
Some say that Chantalle has a **dual** personality because she's really nice some days and not so nice other days.

dubious \DOO bee iss\ (adj.)
arousing doubt, doubtful
The teacher knew that George's excuse about a dog eating his homework was **dubious**, but gave him an extra day to hand it in anyway.

duplicate \DOO plih kit\ (n.)
an exact copy
Timmy made a **duplicate** of his homework assignment just in case a bully stole his on the way to school.

duplicity \doo PLISS ih tee\ (n.)
deception, dishonesty, double-dealing
Ashley was engaging in an act of **duplicity** when she told Shanna she didn't think Derek was hot . . . because she does.

duration \doo RAY shun\ (n.)
period of time that something lasts
After Timmy got slammed in the face with a volleyball during gym, the teacher allowed him to spend the **duration** of the class in the nurse's office.

ebb \EBB\ (v.) -ed, -ing
to fade away, recede
Willow's favorite part of her meditation tape was when the sound of the gong **ebbed** and there was perfect silence.

eccentric \ek SEN trik\ (adj.)
abnormal, unconventional
Some say that Marisol is a bit **eccentric** because sometimes she likes to paint with her own hair.

eclectic \ee KLEK tik\ (adj.)
made up of elements from different sources
Chantalle's closet was an **eclectic** array of clothing, including pieces inspired by the 1980s to the present.

ecstasy \EK stuh see\ (n.)
intense joy or delight
George was filled with **ecstasy** as he participated in a test at the sleep disorder research center—they were actually paying him to sleep!

ecstatic \ek STAT ik\ (adj.)
joyful

Ashley was **ecstatic** when the captain of the football team asked her out in front of the whole senior class.

efficacious \ef ih KAY shus\ (adj.)
effective, efficient

Shanna's **efficacious** study system helped her ace the test.

efficient \ee FISH int\ (adj.)
effective with a minimum of unnecessary effort or waste

Timmy liked to eat his corn on the cob in an **efficient** manner by neatly chomping off one row at a time.

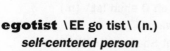

egotist \EE go tist\ (n.)
self-centered person

Everybody knew that Chantalle was an **egotist**, but nobody could believe it when she spent three hours talking about getting her legs waxed.

egregious \i GREE jiss\ (adj.)
conspicuously bad

Josh realized after he handed in his history homework that he had made an **egregious** error: he had copied Timmy's homework word for word that morning, and had also copied Timmy's name onto his paper.

elate \ee LAYT\ (v.) -ed, -ing
to make joyful
Timmy was **elated** when he found out he got
into every Ivy League school he applied to.

elevated \EL uh vay tid\ (adj.)
raised, increased
Ashley felt an **elevated**
sense of nervousness when
she picked up the phone to
call her crush.

eliminate
\ee LIM uh nayt\ (v.) -ed, -ing
get rid of; remove
Paul **eliminated** all the wrong answers to the
test question before he chose the correct one.

elocutionist \el oh Q shun ist\ (n.)
trained public speaker
It was **evident** that Shanna was the real
elocutionist in the class-presidential race and
that her opponent was a sputtering mess.

eloquent \EL uh kwent\ (adj.)
strongly expressing emotion
Paul gave an **eloquent** speech in his English
class about his grandmother and how she led
him to volunteer in a senior citizens' center.

elude \ee LOOD\ (v.) -ed, -ing
evade, escape
Timmy **eluded** Josh by quickly slipping into a stairwell before his tormentor could find him.

elusive \ee LOO siv\ (adj.)
tending to evade
Timmy gripped his camera as he hid in the woods, determined to prove that the **elusive** Big Foot was not a myth.

embellish \em BELL ish\ (v.) -ed, -ing
to ornament; make attractive with decorations or details; add details to a statement
Marisol **embellished** the walls of her room with a string of lights shaped like hot chili peppers.

embezzle \em BEZ ul\ (v.) -ed, -ing
to steal money in violation of a trust
Shanna was surprised to uncover that the school board had **embezzled** thousands of dollars from the library fund and used it for a "business trip" to the Bahamas.

embittered \em BIT urd\ (adj.)
resentful, cynical
Willow found herself **embittered** after she put so much work into her "leather shoes stink" rally at school, and no one showed up.

emend \ee MEND\ (v.) -ed, -ing
to correct a text
George had to **emend** the incorrect price tags
he stamped on the canned peas because the
cost was $.50, not $.05.

emigrate \EM ih grayt\ (v.) -ed, -ing
to leave one country to live in another
As soon as she graduates college, Marisol
plans to **emigrate** from America to live in Italy.

emissary \EM ih ser ee\ (n.)
an agent sent as a representative
Chantalle sent her **emissary**, Shanna, to tell
the cute guy at the other end of the food court
that Chantalle wanted his phone number.

emollient
\ee MOL yent\ (adj.)
having soothing qualities,
especially for skin
Shanna poured the
emollient oils into the
warm bath water to make her
skin super soft.

empathy \EM puh thee\ (n.)
identification with the feelings of others
Having been bullied himself, Timmy felt a strong
empathy for the little kid who was being
pushed around on the playground.

emphatic \em FAT ik\ (adj.)
forceful and definite
When Josh was asked if he wanted to meet his favorite professional basketball player, he answered with an **emphatic** "Yes!"

emulate \EM yoo layt\ (v.) -ed, -ing
to copy, imitate
Shanna often **emulates** her best friend Chantalle, copying her fashion style and dating Chantalle's ex-boyfriends.

enchant \en CHANT\ (v.) -ed, -ing
attract and delight
Paul was **enchanted** by the total hotness of the new girl who had entered his chemistry class, and quickly made room for her to sit next to him.

encompass \en COM pass\ (v.) -ed, -ing
to constitute, include, encircle
Ashley taught the new cheerleaders the Flip-Flop cheer, which **encompassed** everything from basic back flips to a perfect "perma-grin."

encroach \en KROCH\
(v.) -ed, -ing
to infringe, intrude upon
George and Paul went to the movies together, but sat a few seats apart to avoid **encroaching** on each other's snack space.

endemic \en DEM ik\ (adj.)
   belonging to a particular area, inherent
   The students thought the strict dress code was
   unfair because the rule was **endemic** to their
   school only and not to the others in the district.

endorse \en DORSS\ (v.) -ed, -ing
   to give approval to, sanction
   Remarkably, the principal **endorsed** Shanna's
   idea for Senior Cut Day.

endurance \en DOOR uns\ (n.)
   ability to withstand hardships
   It's tough being on the bottom of the
   cheerleader pyramid, so Ashley builds her
   endurance by balancing a sack of potatoes on
   her back for one hour each day.

endure \en DOOR\ (v.) -ed, -ing
   carry on despite hardships
   Derek could not **endure** for one more second
   the boring chamber music concert his parents
   dragged him to, so he left.

enduring \en DOOR ing\ (adj.)
   lasting, continuing
   The enormous statue standing in the courtyard
   is an **enduring** reminder of the school's
   founder . . . as well as a popular resting spot
   for pigeons.

enervate \EN er vayt\ (v.) -ed, -ing
to weaken, drain strength from
George told his mom that he was too tired to take out the garbage because playing video games for three hours had **enervated** him.

enforce \en FORS\ (v.) -ed, -ing
to compel others to adhere or observe
Chantalle **enforced** her authority as "Queen Bee" by having the girls in her clique hang out at the mall with her every Tuesday.

enfranchise \en FRAN chiz\ (v.) -ed, -ing
to give the right to vote to
Willow couldn't wait to become **enfranchised** so she could vote in the next election for the politicians who supported environmental issues.

enhance \in HANSS\ (v.) -ed, -ing
to improve, bring to a greater level of intensity
Chantalle **enhanced** her almond-shaped eyes with two coats of mascara.

enigmatic
\en ig MAT ik\ (adj.)
puzzling
Paul asked out the cute blonde, but her response was so **enigmatic**, he wasn't sure if they had a date or not.

enmity \EN mi tee\ (n.)
hostility, antagonism, ill will
Chantalle couldn't believe the **enmity** she felt toward her best friend, Shanna, when Shanna asked out a guy that Chantalle liked.

ensemble \on SOM bul\ (n.)
group of parts that contribute to a whole single effect
Marisol put together an **ensemble** to wear to her school's art show that was part disco fabulous and part hippie chic.

entangle \en TANG ul\ (v.) -ed, -ing
to complicate, entwine into a confusing mass, involve in
Derek **entangled** himself in a lunchroom argument to try to break it up, but in the end, everyone thought he was the one who started it.

ephemeral \i FEM er il\ (adj.)
momentary, transient, fleeting
Ashley's latest crush was **ephemeral**, thanks to the fact that she saw the guy kissing another girl.

epilogue \EP uh log\ (n.)
concluding section of a literary work
Paul couldn't wait to find out what happened to the characters in the book, so he skipped to the end, read the **epilogue**, and spoiled the surprise.

epistolary \eh PIS tuh ler ee\ (n.)
associated with letter writing
Even though **epistolary** discourses are a thing of the past, Marisol thinks it's romantic to correspond with boyfriends through letters.

epitaph \EH pih taf\ (n.)
engraving on a tombstone, literary piece for a dead person
Although she didn't know him well, Willow wrote an extensive **epitaph** for the caterpillar she accidentally squashed on the way to school.

equitable \EH kwi tuh bul\ (adj.)
fair; just and impartial
Ashley could come up with only one **equitable** solution for the two football players who were fighting over her. She would date them both.

eradicate \ee RAD ih kayt\ (v.) -ed, -ing
to erase or wipe out
Paul wished trigonometry could be **eradicated**, so he would never have to study for another test.

erasure \ee RAY shur\ (n.)
the act or instance of erasing
Timmy swore his name wasn't on the guest list due to an accidental **erasure**, but that still didn't get him into the party.

erosion \ee ROW zhin\ (n.)
the process or condition of wearing away
Shanna joined Willow in the fight to save the beaches from **erosion** because if she didn't, she might not have a place to wear her bikini in a few years.

erratic \ee RAT ik\ (adj.)
unpredictable, inconsistent
Paul made his friends laugh with his **erratic** movements on the dance floor.

erroneously \ee ROWN ee us lee\ (adv.)
mistakenly, inaccurately
Shanna apologized when she **erroneously** accused her little sister of taking her favorite Diggity Dawgz CD.

espouse \eh SPOWZ\ (v.) -ed, -ing
to support or advocate; to marry
When asked what would make the world a better place, Chantalle **espoused** free manicures for everyone.

essential \E sen shul\ (n.)
something fundamental or indispensable
Josh is a little embarrassed that he still needs his teddy bear, but it's **essential** for a good night's sleep.

ethical \ETH ih kul\ (adj.)
moral, right-minded
George knew it wasn't **ethical** to peek at the test answers on the teacher's desk...so he looked at only one answer.

ethos \EE thos\ (n.)
beliefs or character of a group
In accordance with the **ethos** of her clique, Chantalle wears the color pink because she believes it's good luck.

eulogy \YOO luh jee\ (n.)
high praise for a person who has died
Timmy wrote a **eulogy** for his dog, Marbles, who had been with the family for 14 years.

euphoria \yoo FOR ee uh\ (n.)
a great feeling of happiness or well-being
Derek was overcome with **euphoria** when an agent saw his band's show and told them that he'd make them stars.

evade \ee VAYD\ (v.) -ed, -ing
to avoid, dodge
When George's parents asked him how he did on his science test, he **evaded** the question as best he could before admitting that he had gotten a C-.

evaluate \ee VAL yoo ayt\ (v.) -ed, -ing
to examine or judge carefully
The English teacher told the class that she
would **evaluate** the students' essays based on
tone, grammar, and content.

evanescent \ev in ESS nt\ (adj.)
momentary, transient, short-lived
George's liking his new job at the clothing store
was **evanescent** because he soon realized
there was no place to nap during breaks.

evaporate \ee VAP uh rayt\ (v.) -ed, -ing
to vanish quickly
Timmy's smile **evaporated** when he realized
that the crowd was not laughing with him,
but at him.

evenhanded \ee ven HAND id\ (adj.)
fair, impartial
Ashley thought she could be **evenhanded** when
picking girls for the cheerleading team, but she
wound up choosing all of her friends instead.

exacerbate
\ig ZAS ur bayt\ (v.) -ed, -ing
*to aggravate, intensify the
bad qualities of*
Unfortunately, George ate
cabbage for lunch, which
exacerbated the gas in
his stomach.

exacting \eg ZAK ting\ (adj.)
requiring a lot of care or attention
Dating Chantalle is an **exacting** task because
if you give her too much or too little attention,
she'll drop you like a hot potato.

exaggerate \eg ZAJ uh rayt\ (v.) -ed, -ing
*to represent something as greater than it
actually is*
George stubbed his toe and **exaggerated** the
pain he was feeling so that his girlfriend would
rub his feet.

exalt \eg ZALT\ (v.) -ed, -ing
to glorify or honor
"We're the best!" Ashley cheered, **exalting** the
soccer team who, until their last game, hadn't
won all year.

exasperation \eg zas pe RAY shun\ (n.)
irritation
Josh, unable to hide his **exasperation** at his
team's fumbling the football, yelled at the
coach to put him in the game.

exception \ek SEP shun\ (n.)
a case that doesn't conform to a generalization
With the **exception** of *I Love My Puppy*, all of
the band Snakebite's alternative rock songs
are about overcoming the many injustices
in the world.

exclude \ek SKLOOD\ (v.) -ed, -ing
to prevent from being accepted or included
Timmy knew he was a bit nerdy at times, but
that was no reason to **exclude** him from the
cool group . . . was it?

exculpate \EK skul payt\ (v.) -ed, -ing
to clear of blame or fault, vindicate
Ashley was accused of taking Shanna's pocket
mirror, but was soon **exculpated** when Shanna
noticed Chantalle staring at her reflection in it
across the room.

excursion \ek SKUHR zhen\ (n.)
short journey, usually for pleasure
Shanna accompanied Chantalle on her
excursion to the mall even though Shanna had
already spent her allowance for that week.

exemplary \egg ZEM pluh ree\ (adj.)
outstanding, an example to others
The teacher told the unruly students that Paul's
exemplary behavior was something to learn from.
Of course, she hadn't seen Paul throw the paper
airplane across the room five minutes earlier.

exemplify \eg ZEMP lih fi\ (v.) -ied, -ing
to show by example
Josh used Timmy's boxer shorts to **exemplify**
the precise way of stringing underwear up
a flagpole.

exhortation \eg zor TAY shun\ (n.)
speech that advises or pleads
Willow's **exhortation** did not get the kids to help the plight of the dung beetle, but it did result in students putting beetles in her locker.

exorbitant \eg ZORB ih tant\ (adj.)
extravagant, greater than reasonable
Because of the **exorbitant** prices of oil-based paints, Marisol decided to switch to watercolors.

expedite \EK spe diyt\ (v.) -ed, -ing
to speed up the progress of
Derek would not sacrifice the quality of his band's music just to **expedite** the release of their first single.

expertise \ek spur TEEZ\ (adj.)
skill or knowledge in a particular area
Timmy called the talk-radio show to show off his **expertise** on that morning's topic: Extraterrestrials Living Among Us.

explanatory \ek SPLAN uh tor ee\ (adj.)
serving to make clear
The school sent George's parents an **explanatory** note about how George's continual absence might result in him not graduating.

exploit \ek SPLOYT\ (v.) -ed, -ing
take advantage of
Chantalle **exploited** her friendship with Paul by getting him to do her math homework for her.

expropriate \ek SPRO pree ayt\ (v.) -ed, -ing
forcibly take one's property
Josh **expropriated** Timmy's seat in the lunchroom by tossing Timmy's backpack onto the next table and sitting in his chair.

expurgate \EK spur gayt\ (v.) -ed, -ing
to censor
Timmy's mom couldn't **expurgate** the R-rated movies from the cable television channels, so she put a lock on the cable box instead.

extant \EK stant\ (adj.)
still in existence
Chantalle was horrified when she discovered that the pictures of her with braces from middle school were **extant**—and being passed around her math class.

extensive \ek STEN siv\ (adj.)
large in range, comprehensive
Chantalle yawned when her mom gave her a long and **extensive** lecture on the virtues of being humble.

extenuating \ek STEN yoo ayt ing\ (adj.)
partially excusing
Shanna was not grounded for missing curfew because of the **extenuating** circumstances: her car broke down and she had to walk all the way home.

exterminate
\ek STUR mu nayt\ (v.) -ed, -ing
destroy completely, annihilate
Josh cheered when the action hero single-handedly **exterminated** the bad guys in the movie.

external \ek STUR nel\ (adj.)
exterior, outer part
Paul liked Marisol not only because of her **external** beauty, but because she was beautiful inside as well.

extol \ek STOL\ (v.) -led, -ling
to praise
The art teacher **extolled** Marisol's painting, saying that it was the best one on display.

extravagant \ek STRAV uh gent\ (adj.)
unreasonably high, exorbitant
Josh preferred a nice juicy burger from the Burger Barn to the **extravagant** meals his parents ate at fancy restaurants.

extreme \ek STREEM\ (adj.)
very intense, of the greatest severity, excessive
Paul wondered if offering the vice principal a stick of trick gum that would turn his mouth black was a little **extreme**, but he did it anyway.

extricate \EK stri kayt\ (v.) -ed, -ing
to free from, disentangle
Ashley grunted in the dressing room as she tried to **extricate** herself from the weird fishnet top.

extroverted \EK stro ver tid\ (adj.)
outgoing, easily talks to others
Shanna was elected class president because she was the most **extroverted** candidate and made it a point to talk to every student.

exultant \eg ZUL tent\ (adj.)
triumphant
Timmy cheered, **exultant**, after finally tricking Josh the bully into a locker before Josh shoved him into one.

fabricated
\fab rih KAY tid\ (adj.)
constructed, invented;
faked, falsified
George **fabricated** an excuse for
missing choir practice because he could-
n't tell the teacher that he didn't feel like going.

facade \fuh SOD\ (n.)
face, front; mask, superficial appearance
Timmy put on a **facade** of not caring if the cool
crowd liked him, but inside he really did care.

facile \FA sul\ (adj.)
skilled, adept; requiring skill
Willow was amazingly **facile** at getting people
involved in causes.

factual \FAK choo ul\ (adj.)
real
The teacher had a hunch that Timmy had let
Josh copy his homework, but she did not have
any **factual** evidence.

fallacious \fu LAY shuss\ (adj.)
wrong, unsound, illogical
Ashley refuted the **fallacious** statement that she could not be spontaneous if her life depended on it by picking a random boy in the mall and kissing him on the lips.

falsify \FAL sih fiy\ (v.) -ied, -ing
misrepresent, state untruthfully
George considered **falsifying** the D on his report card by changing it to a B because he was afraid to show it to his parents.

fanfare \FAN fayr\ (n.)
a showy public display
Josh enjoyed the **fanfare** the football team received at the start of every game.

fathom \FAH thom\ (v.) -ed, -ing
comprehend, penetrate the meaning of
Chantalle could not **fathom** why her mom would actually choose to wear her hair in a beehive.

favoritism \FAV uh rih tizm\ (n.)
one-sidedness, partiality to one side
The teacher clearly showed **favoritism** for the girls in the class when she gave only the boys homework.

feign \FAYN\ (v.) -ed, -ing
to pretend, give a false impression;
to invent falsely
Paul **feigns** disinterest around Marisol to hide
the fact that he really, really, really likes her.

felicitous \feh LIH sih tus\ (adj.)
suitable, appropriate;
well-spoken
Willow made a **felicitous**
speech at the Save the
Seagulls event, which
contributed to the success
of the fundraiser.

feral \FER ul\ (adj.)
wild, brutish
One might say that Josh, a bully and a jock, is
more **feral** than bookish Timmy and his friends
in the poetry club.

fertile \FIR tul\ (adj.)
highly productive, prolific
Willow's whimsical art is a direct result of her
fertile imagination.

fickle \FIK ul\ (adj.)
erratically unstable about affections
Chantalle is **fickle** when it comes to nail polish;
she's always changing her mind about which
color she likes best.

fidelity \fih DEL ih tee\ (n.)
loyalty, faithfulness
Shanna knows that she can rely on her little sister's **fidelity** as long as Shanna continues to give her ten bucks a week.

figurative \FIG ur uh tiv\ (adj.)
metaphorical, symbolic
Shanna told Timmy that she'd date him "when pigs fly," which is a **figurative** way of saying "never."

finite \FI niyt\ (adj.)
having bounds, limited
Although Timmy loved eating egg salad, he learned that six was the **finite** number of days he could eat it in a row before getting sick of it.

firebrand \FIYR brand\ (n.)
one who stirs up trouble
The school administration thinks Derek is a **firebrand** because he sometimes wears a spiky black collar around his neck.

fission \FISH in\ (n.)
process of splitting into two parts
Timmy stared through his microscope in awe as Sparkey, his pet amoeba, went through the process of **fission** and split into two amoebas.

flabbergast \FLAB ur gast\ (v.) -ed, -ing
astound, surprise
Shanna was **flabbergasted** when her parents gave her a car for her birthday.

flagrant \FLAY grent\ (adj.)
outrageous, shameless
The couple's **flagrant** display of affection in the hallway led to a trip to detention hall.

flank \FLANK\ (v.) -ed, -ing
to put on the sides of
Ashley smiled and waved to her friends who were **flanking** the school hallway as she walked past.

flaunt \FLAWNT\ (v.) -ed, -ing
to show off
Timmy **flaunted** the gold medal that he won in the Academic Olympics all over school.

flaw \FLAW\ (n.)
imperfection, defect
Some students thought the birthmark on the teacher's cheek was a **flaw**, but Marisol saw it as a work of art on a blank canvas.

flee \FLEE\ (v.) -ed, -ing
run away from, escape
The kids **fled** the house party when the police arrived at the door.

flippancy \FLIP an see\ (adj.)
casualness, inappropriate pertness
Ashley couldn't stand the **flippancy** of the other cheerleaders. Didn't they know that pumping up a crowd was serious business?

florid \FLAW rid\ (adj.)
ruddy, flushed; gaudy, extremely ornate
George's face was hot and **florid** after he finished the required three-mile run on the track.

flourish \FLUR ish\ (v.) -ed, -ing
prosper, thrive
Shanna's academic career was **flourishing** in her small high school and she hoped to do as well at a large university.

foil \FOYL\ (n.)
something used to contrast with something else
George's stomach churned when his boss said the "employee of the month" at the clothing store was his **foil** for evaluating George's work performance.

foreshadow \FOR shah dow\ (v.) -ed, -ing
to indicate beforehand
Shanna hoped her landslide election as senior class president **foreshadowed** her future landslide election as president of the United States.

forge \FORJ\ (v.) -ed, -ing
to advance gradually but steadily
Although she thought yoga was very hard, Willow **forged** through the rest of her workout.

forgery \FORJ uh ree\ (n.)
something counterfeit or fraudulent, pertaining to a document
Chantalle said that signing her mother's name on a credit card receipt was not **forgery** because her mother gave her permission to do it.

forlorn \for LORN\ (adj.)
dreary, deserted; unhappy; hopeless, depressing
Derek felt **forlorn** at the prospect of telling his band that his agent wanted him to go solo.

formidable \FOR mid uh bul\ (adj.)
arousing fear or dread; inspiring awe or wonder; difficult to undertake
Timmy was up against a **formidable** opponent at the chess match, but managed to keep his cool and win.

fortitude \FOR ti tood\ (n.)
strength of mind
It's not that Willow had the **fortitude** to hold her yoga pose for an hour straight, it's that she couldn't get out of the pose without someone coming to help her.

forum \FOR um\ (n.)
public place for discussion; a public discussion
Shanna, the class president, held an open
forum in the auditorium to discuss student
issues.

fraud \FRAWD\ (n.)
deception, hoax, imposter, phony
Ashley felt like a total **fraud** in chorus class as
she lip-synched the words to a song when she
couldn't remember the melody.

frivolous \FRIV uh luss\ (adj.)
petty, trivial; flippant, silly
Willow's parents think that her protesting is just
a **frivolous** phase, but Willow contends that
she is strongly committed to each and every
issue.

frolicsome
\FROL ik sum\ (adj.)
frisky, playful
The first snowfall put
George in a **frolicsome**
mood, so he ran
outside to build a snowman.

frugal \FROO gul\ (adj.)
thrifty, cheap
Ashley is **frugal** when it comes to lip gloss and
buys the cheapest brand on the market.

fundamental \fun da MEN tul\ (adj.)
basic, essential
Marisol tried to explain to her parents that one
of the **fundamental** rules of art is that there
are no rules.

futile \FYOO tiyl\ (adj.)
useless; hopeless
George realized that studying further for his
Spanish test was **futile**, so he decided to play
video games instead.

G

gargantuan
\gar GAN shoo in\ (adj.)
giant, tremendous
Chantalle needs a **gargantuan**-sized closet to store all of her shoes in.

garish \GAH rish\ (adj.)
gaudy, glaring
Marisol loved the **garish** candelabra that she bought at the flea market, but her mother said it was too gaudy to display in the dining room.

generalize \JEN er uh liyz\ (v.) -ed, -ing
reduce to a general form
Chantalle is clearly **generalizing** when she says that all jocks are stupid.

genial \JEEN yul\ (adj.)
pleasant, friendly, gracious
Ashley's **genial** manner often rubs off on the people around her.

gibber \JI buhr\ (v.) -ed, -ing
prattle unintelligibly
Ashley's baby cousin **gibbered** happily
whenever Ashley picked him up.

glacier \GLAY sher\ (n.)
slow-moving, large mass of ice
Willow asked her parents to take her on a
cruise to Alaska so that she could get a look at
enormous **glaciers** up close.

glossy \GLAW see\ (adj.)
shiny, showy, sleek
Josh was psyched when
his dad tossed him the
keys to his **glossy** red
sports car.

glutton \GLUT in\ (n.)
person who eats and drinks excessively
It was well known that George was a **glutton**,
but the three hamburgers, six orders of fries,
thirteen cupcakes, and a Diet Coke was a lot
of food even for him to eat.

goad \GOAD\ (v.) -ed, -ing
to prod or urge
When Shanna was younger, she used to
goad her little sister to eat bugs from their
mom's garden.

gourmand \goor MOND\ (n.)
glutton; lover of fine food
Marisol thought her date was a **gourmand** when he took her to a fancy French restaurant and answered all of her questions about the intricacies of fine dining.

gracious \GRAY shus\ (adj.)
kind, compassionate, warm-hearted, courteous
Ashley was quite **gracious** when the two-hundred-pound football player accidentally stepped on her foot.

grandiose \GRAN dee ohss\ (adj.)
magnificent and imposing; exaggerated and pretentious
Paul made a **grandiose** gesture of pulling out Marisol's chair for her when she came into the classroom.

gratuity \gruh too ih tee\ (n.)
something given voluntarily, tip
The bellboy held out his hand and Derek slapped him five, unaware that the guy expected a **gratuity** for dragging Derek's luggage up six flights of stairs.

gravity \GRAH vih tee\ (adj.)
importance, seriousness
Josh laughed when he was pulled over for speeding, but it took only one stern look from the state trooper for Josh to realize the **gravity** of the situation.

grove \GROHV\ (n.)
a group of trees
Willow loves to lie under the trees in the apple **grove** and contemplate the meaning of life.

grudgingly
\GRUDJ ing lee\ (adj.)
reluctantly, resentfully
Marisol **grudgingly** agreed to be in the school fashion show—but only if she could approve her outfit in advance.

gruff \GRUF\ (adj.)
brusque, stern, harsh
Josh ignored his father's **gruff** voice when he asked if Josh was going to clean his room sometime this year.

hackneyed
\HAK need\ (adj.)
clichéd, worn out by overuse
Chantalle thought the "roses are red, violets are blue" poem she received from a boy in her math class was totally **hackneyed**, and threw it out.

hallmark \HAUL mark\ (n.)
specific feature, characteristc
A cheery disposition and gymnastic ability are two **hallmarks** of a great cheerleader.

harangue \hu RANG\ (n.)
pompous speech, tirade
George patiently listened to Willow's **harangue** about mad cow disease as he chowed down on a gigantic cheeseburger.

harass \hu RASS\ (v.) -ed, -ing
irritate, torment
Timmy **harassed** his parents until they finally agreed to buy him a professional microscope.

haughty \HAW tee\ (adj.)
arrogant and condescending
George did not like the **haughty** attitude
Chantalle was giving him, so he "accidentally"
tripped and spilled his milk on her sweater.

hazardous \HA zer duss\ (adj.)
dangerous, risky, perilous
Willow panicked when she spotted **hazardous**
waste materials in the school stairwell...until
she realized that it was only someone's
squashed tuna salad sandwich.

heckler \HEK ler\ (n.)
someone who tries to embarrass and annoy others
During her speech to the students, Shanna shot
down a **heckler** in the audience with a quick
comeback.

hedonism \HEE doh nizm\ (n.)
pursuit of pleasure as a goal
Chantalle spent six hours getting pampered at
a spa, calling it her day of **hedonism**.

heed \HEED\ (v.)
-ed, -ing
pay attention to
After being pulled over
for speeding, Paul
chose to **heed** the
officer's advice and
drive at the speed limit.

heinous \HAY nes\ (adj.)
shocking, wicked, terrible
Ashley thought Josh's constant teasing of Timmy was completely **heinous**, yet she did nothing to stop it.

hesitant \HE zih tent\ (adj.)
doubtful, reluctant
Marisol was **hesitant** to discuss the inspiration for her next art project with her competitive classmate.

hierarchy \HIYR ar kee\ (n.)
ranking system of authority groups
As senior class president, Shanna is at the top of the the student government **hierarchy**; the vice president, treasurer, and secretary all report to her.

hindrance \HIN drins\ (n.)
impediment, clog; stumbling block
Timmy faints at the sight of blood, which could be a **hindrance** if he wants to become a brain surgeon someday.

hindsight \HIYND siyt\ (n.)
perception of events after they happen
In **hindsight**, Paul realized that you should never talk about people in the bathroom because you never know who is in a stall listening.

hodgepodge \HOJ poj\ (n.)
jumble, mixture of assorted objects
Marisol pasted a **hodgepodge** of toiletries onto a white toilet seat and called it "The Beauty Bowl."

hoist \HOYST\ (v.) -ed, -ing
lift, raise
Josh was **hoisted** into the air by his teammates after hitting the winning home run for his baseball team.

humane \hyoo MAYN\ (adj.)
merciful, kind
When Willow found a box of three puppies at her doorstep, she did the **humane** thing and found each one a home.

hypocrisy \hih POK rih see\ (n.)
claiming of beliefs that one doesn't really possess
Willow considered it **hypocrisy** when students said they cared about animals, but continued to eat meat.

hypothesis \hi POTH a siss\ (n.)
assumption, theory requiring proof
Timmy's **hypothesis** about bullies is that they need to push people down to feel good about themselves.

idealist
\iy DEEL ist\ (n.)
someone that is unrealistic and impractical in their beliefs
The reason that Willow pursues so many causes is that she is an **idealist**.

illegible \ih LEJ ih bul\ (adj.)
unreadable, undecipherable
Ashley appreciated George lending her his history notes, but unfortunately his handwriting was **illegible** and she couldn't figure out what he had written.

illuminate \il LOOM ih nayt\ (v.) -ed, -ing
fill with light
Timmy's imitation Star Wars lightsaber **illuminated** his room when he switched it on.

illusory \ih LOOZ uh ree\ (adj.)
unreal, deceptive
As Josh walked home from school, he realized that the fast-food joint down the block was **illusory**, and he had only his empty stomach to blame for the hallucination.

illustrate \IL uh strayt\
(v.) -ed, -ing
provide an example, explain
George's mom used the six-hour videotape of her son watching television to **illustrate** the point that he was a couch potato.

imitate \im ih TAYT\ (v.) -ed, -ing
copy, impersonate
Knock-off designers often **imitate** the popular designs of expensive brands when creating their own clothing lines.

immoderate \im MOD ih rit\ (adj.)
excessive
Ashley's mother did not approve of the **immoderate** amount of soda her daughter drank and limited her to one can per day.

immunity \im MYOO ni tee\ (n.)
invulnerability, exemption
The seniors all skipped school on Senior Cut Day because the principal had offered them **immunity** from punishment.

immutable \im MYOOT uh bul\ (adj.)
unchangeable, invariable
Willow thought her carnivorous parents were **immutable** and was quite surprised when they stopped eating meat at her request.

impassioned \im PASH ind\ (adj.)
with great feeling
Shanna made an **impassioned** plea to the principal to use school funds to fix the bleachers in the gymnasium.

impassive \im PASS iv\ (adj.)
showing no emotion
The principal listened **impassively** to the student's lame excuse for starting a food fight before declaring him suspended.

impenitent \im PEN ih tent\ (adj.)
not remorseful
Shanna's **impenitent** behavior for missing curfew, yet again, outraged her parents and she was grounded for three weeks.

imperceptible \im per SEP ti buhl\ (adj.)
subtle, difficult to perceive
Even though her burp was almost **imperceptible**, Ashley felt mortified for doing it in front of her friends.

implausible \im PLAW zuh bul\ (adj.)
improbable, inconceivable
No matter how many times Timmy tried to prove he was abducted by aliens, his friends found the story highly **implausible**.

implement \IMP luh ment\ (v.) -ed, -ing
carry out, put into effect
Chantalle was thrilled when her parents decided to **implement** a higher allowance for her per week.

impotent \IM puh tent\ (adj.)
powerless, ineffective, lacking strength
No matter how much they practiced, the swim team was **impotent** against the reigning state champs.

impressionable \im PRESH in uh bul\ (adj.)
easily influenced or affected
The freshmen were highly **impressionable**—if the upperclassmen told them Brussels sprouts were cool, the freshmen would eat them for a week straight.

impugn \im PYOON\ (v.) -ed, -ing
to call into question, attack verbally
Derek impugned his manager's **integrity** when he found out the guy had cheated another singer out of thousands of dollars.

impute \im PYOOT\ (v.) -ed, -ing
to attribute, to credit
Marisol **imputed** Chantalle's good looks to nice makeup and a quality hair dryer, not natural beauty.

inaccessible \in ak SES uh bul\ (adj.)
unreachable, unapproachable
Most kids thought the principal's office was
inaccessible, but Paul found a way in through
an air vent in the library.

inarticulate \in ar TIK yoo lit\ (adj.)
incomprehensible, unable to speak clearly
As he stared at the confused faces of his
history teacher and his classmates, Josh had a
sinking feeling that his oral report on the New
Deal was completely **inarticulate**.

inauspicious \in aw SPISH is\ (adj.)
unfavorable
Chantalle's cell phone always rings at
the most **inauspicious** times, like when
she has her hands full of shopping bags
or when she's in the bathroom.

incantation \in kan TAY shun\ (n.)
a verbal spell
Willow burned a bundle of sage, waved it
around, and said a quiet **incantation** as she
sanctified the desk in her room as her official
studying place.

incidental \in sih DEN tul\ (adj.)
minor, casual
Derek did not take into account the **incidental**
necessities of a road trip—like gas—and had to
call his mom to come get him when the car died.

incisive \in SY siv\ (adj.)
perceptive, penetrating
The teacher was surprised when George raised his hand and gave an **incisive** comment on the American Revolution. Unfortunately for George, it was during math class.

incompetent \in KOM puh tent\ (adj.)
unqualified, inept
Marisol thought her art teacher was totally **incompetent** because he didn't even know who Picasso was.

incongruous \in KONG roo us\ (adj.)
inappropriate, incompatible
The editor of *Hot for Hunting* magazine deemed Willow's letter to the editor, which demanded that he denounce hunting, **incongruous** with the interests of his readers.

inconsequential \in con se KWEN shul\ (adj.)
unimportant, trivial
Willow's parents considered Willow's grades **inconsequential** as long as they knew she was trying her best.

inconsistent \in kon SIS tent\ (adj.)
contradictory
George told his gym teacher that he exercised every day, but his statement was **inconsistent** with the size of his stomach.

inconspicuous \in con SPIK yoo us\ (adj.)
not easily noticeable
Shanna was sick of her sister reading her diary so she put a fake journal out in the open on her nightstand and her real one in an **inconspicuous** spot on her bookshelf.

incriminate
\in KRIM uh nayt\ (v.) -ed, -ing
to *accuse of a crime, implicate*
Willow swore that she didn't eat meat, but the half-eaten burger in her hand was quite **incriminating**.

incumbent \in KUM bent\ (adj.)
holding a specified office, often political
Shanna isn't the only **incumbent** officer in the school; there are also the vice president, secretary, and treasurer.

indebted \in DET id\ (adj.)
obligated to someone else, beholden
Shanna is **indebted** to Chantalle because Shanna *so* owes Chantalle for getting her a date with the cute foreign-exchange student.

indecorous \in DEK uh rus\ (adj.)
improper, lacking good taste
George's girlfriend was embarrassed by his **indecorous** behavior in front of her parents.

indefatigable \in de FAT ih gu bul\ (adj.)
never tired
Josh seemed **indefatigable** as he shot basket
after basket without even breaking a sweat.

indefinite \in DEF in it\ (adj.)
vague, undecided, unclear
George swore he was going to join a gym,
though the start date was **indefinite**....

indeterminate \in de TER mi nit\ (adj.)
vague, unknown, imprecise
Willow marveled at the **indeterminate** number
of causes she could support at one time.

indignant \in DIG nint\ (adj.) *angry,
incensed, offended*
Chantalle became **indignant** when she learned
that Derek had called her selfish and spoiled.

indiscernible
\in di SER nu bul\ (adj.)
difficult to detect
Ashley's new black
pants are **indiscernible**
from her old black pants.

indiscretion \in dis KRESH
un\ (n.)
lack of prudence, mistake
Josh's **indiscretion** on the football field cost
his team the playoffs.

indiscriminate
\in dis KRIM uh nit\ (adj.)
not based on careful distinctions, chaotic
Since Derek lost his **indiscriminate** bet, he was forced to play guitar at his four-year-old cousin's birthday party while dressed as a purple dinosaur.

indistinct \in di STINKT\ (adj.)
vague, unclear
After years of being a high school bully, Josh's nerdy middle school days became **indistinct** in his mind.

indomitable \in DOM ih tu bul\ (adj.)
fearless, unconquerable
Josh thought he was **indomitable**, until little Timmy stuck out his foot and tripped him.

induce \in DOOS\ (v.) -ed, -ing
to persuade; bring about
Paul **induced** laughter from his friends with his classroom antics.

industrious \in DUS tree us\ (adj.)
hardworking, diligent
After several weeks of being an **industrious** tree hugger, Willow decided to take a break and get down with her bad self on the dance floor at a friend's party.

ineffable \in EF uh bul\ (adj.)
indescribable, inexpressible
Chantalle found Marisol's outrageous fashion statement to be **ineffable**, so she took a picture with her camera phone and sent it to her friends.

inefficacious \in ef ih KAY shus\ (adj.)
ineffective, incompetent
No matter how hard he tried, George's effort to get to work on time was **inefficacious**.

inefficient
\in ih FISH ent\ (adj.)
wasteful of resources, time, or energy
Willow wrote her social studies paper on the **inefficient** use of toilet water in the United States.

inept \in EPT\ (adj.)
clumsy, awkward; foolish, nonsensical
Although Marisol was terrific at producing abstract paintings, she was completely **inept** at sculpture.

inevitable \in EV ih tu bul\ (adj.)
certain, unavoidable
Marisol's passion for art was so strong, it was **inevitable** that she would go to the finest art school in the country.

inexorable \in EK sur uh bul\ (adj.)
inflexible, unyielding
Chantalle found her parents' **inexorable** attitude toward changing the house rules to be unfair.

infinite \IN fu nit\ (adj.)
unlimited, boundless
Shanna did not have the **infinite** patience required for baby-sitting her neighbor's noisy kids, and quit after the first day.

inflammatory \in FLAM uh tor ee\ (adj.)
arousing passion, usually anger
Willow's **inflammatory** remarks about the girl wearing fur-lined gloves in the schoolyard caused the girl to pour her latte over Willow's head.

inflation \in FLAY shun\ (n.)
undue amplification
Although the students knew that the gossip flying through the halls was an **inflation** of the truth, they liked to pass it on anyway.

inflexible \in FLEK su bul\ (adj.)
rigid, unbending
Despite his parents' objections, George remained **inflexible** in his decision not to clean his room.

infusion \in FYOO zhin\ (n.)
the introduction of, the addition of
Josh told the coach he got an **infusion** of energy from eating candy bars.

inhibit \in HIB it\ (v.) -ed, -ing
to hold back, prevent, restrain
Marisol was a bit **inhibited** at the start of the dance but later felt free enough to dance on top of a table.

innumerable \ih NOOM ur uh bul\ (adj.)
too many to be counted
Willow's mom sighed as she picked up yet another of her daughter's **innumerable** "Save the..." buttons scattered around the house.

inordinate \in OR di net\ (adj.)
excessive, immoderate
Shanna thought it was strange that every time she used a ballpoint pen she wound up with an **inordinate** amount of ink stains on her pants.

inscription \in SKRIP shun\ (n.)
engraving
George laughed at the **inscription** on the watch in the lost and found box; it said, "To Hunny, Luv Bunny."

insidious \in SID ee us\ (adj.)
subtly harmful, beguiling, alluring
Chantalle's **insidious** remarks about Shanna's straight, boring hair led Shanna to get a perm.

insightful \in SIYT ful\ (adj.)
clever, perceptive, intuitive
Ashley showed her college application essay to her English teacher, hoping he'd have some **insightful** comments on how she could improve it.

insinuate \in SIN yoo ayt\ (v.) -ed, -ing
to suggest, say indirectly, imply
Josh didn't pick up it on when Timmy **insinuated** that Josh wouldn't be smart enough to get a job after college.

insolence \IN su luns\ (n.)
rudeness, impertinence
Chantalle was angered by the **insolence** of the sales clerk after he found out her credit card was declined.

instantaneous \in sten TAY nee us\ (adj.)
immediate, without delay
Timmy almost always gets an **instantaneous** response when he e-mails his friends because his friends are almost always online.

insular \IN syu lar\ (adj.)
isolated, provincial
Marisol can't wait to leave behind her **insular** life in high school and see the world.

integrate \IN tih grayt\
   (v.) -ed, -ing
   to incorporate, unite
   Willow tried to **integrate** tofu into her parents' diet, but her father said, "No way."

integrity
   \in TEG rih tee\ (n.)
   decency, honesty, wholeness
   Josh showed a shred of **integrity** when he gave Timmy a ride home during the rainstorm.

intellectual \in te LEK shoo ul\ (n.)
   intelligent, scholarly
   Shanna thought George was surprisingly **intellectual** for a guy who watches cartoons every day.

intemperate \in TEM per ut\ (adj.)
   not moderate
   Although Willow and her father's political views are both **intemperate**, they are on opposite sides of the spectrum.

interlocutor \in ter LOK yu tur\ (n.)
   someone taking part in a dialogue
   Chantalle wasn't the only one talking about Marisol's outfit that morning; surprisingly, Ashley was an **interlocutor** as well.

interlude \IN ter lood\ (n.)
an intervening period of time
Paul was glad for the **interlude** between the first and second acts of the boring play, so he could leave without disrupting the actors.

interminable \in TER mi nu bul\ (adj.)
endless
The length of the history class was the same as every other, but the day's dull topic made it seem **interminable**.

intransigent \in TRAN zu jent\ (adj.)
uncompromising, refusing to be reconciled
Marisol was **intransigent** about never ever working for a corporate establishment because she thought that by doing so she would be selling out as an artist.

intrepid \in TREP id\ (adj.)
fearless
Ashley was surprised to learn that despite his scrawny stature, Timmy was an **intrepid** rock climber.

intricate \IN tri kit\ (adj.)
elaborate, complex
Willow was mesmerized in science class as she watched the black widow spider spin an **intricate** web to catch its prey.

intrusion \in TROO zhin\ (n.)
invasion of another's privacy
Shanna complained about her little sister's constant **intrusion** into her room.

inundate \IN un dayt\
(v.) -ed, -ing
to cover with water;
to overwhelm
Ever since Timmy ordered that mini-robot from the Internet he's been **inundated** with thousands of pop-up ads offering great deals on other robots.

invariable \in VAR ee uh bul\ (adj.)
constant, unchanging
When his science teacher asked for an **invariable** law of nature, Timmy volunteered that on Earth, the sun rises and sets every day.

inventory \IN vin tohr ee\ (n.)
the quantity of goods on hand
Chantalle checked the **inventory** of purses in her closet and realized that she was missing her pink one.

investigate \in VES tih gayt\ (v.) -ed, -ing
examine, look into
Shanna **investigated** the top twenty colleges in the country and applied to the ones on the list that were close to home.

investment \in VEST mint\ (n.)
a commitment of time, support, or money
Timmy's **investment** in Spanish lessons paid
off when he was able to speak with the
exchange student from Spain.

inviolable \in VY uh lu bul\ (adj.)
safe from violation or assault
After a tough day of protesting, Willow retreats to
her house where she feels safe and **inviolable**.

iridescent
\ih ri DES ent\ (adj.)
showing many colors
After the heavy rainfall,
George spotted an **iridescent** rainbow and won-
dered if there was a pot of
gold at the end of it.

irony \I ur nee\ (n.)
incongruity between expectations and actualities
Derek seethed at the **irony** of leaving his band
for a solo record deal; now Snakebite had a
record deal of their own, while Derek sat at home
with his mom watching "Wheel of Fortune."

irrational \ih RASH ih null\ (adj.)
illogical, nonsensical, unreasonable
Even though Timmy is very allergic to
strawberries, he has an **irrational** desire
to eat them.

irresolute \ih REZ uh loot\ (adj.)
undecided; indecisive, fickle
Chantalle was so **irresolute** about the outfit she wanted to wear that morning, that by the time she picked one out, she was late for school.

irreverent \ir REV er ent\ (adj.)
disrespectful, gently or humorously mocking
The students laughed at Josh's **irreverent** comment in class, but the teacher thought the topic of world hunger was too serious to joke about.

isolated \I suh lay tid\ (adj.)
solitary, singular
Shanna realized that her decision to wear knickers to school was not a cool fashion statement, but instead an **isolated** case of bad judgment.

jaded \JAY ded\ (adj.)
tired by excess or overuse; slightly cynical
Ashley told anyone she met who had a **jaded** attitude to turn that frown upside down.

jeopardize \JEP er diyz\ (v.) -ed, -ing
endanger, expose to injury
Shanna hoped her late-breaking case of chicken pox wasn't going to **jeopardize** her perfect GPA.

jest \JEST\ (v.) -ed, -ing
to act playfully, ridicule
"Surely you **jest**," Chantalle said, when her mother asked Chantalle to accompany her to the thrift store.

jollity \JOL ih tee\ (n.)
cheerfulness, liveliness; celebration
Ashley's **jollity** seemed insincere to some students because there was no way someone could smile 24/7.

jubilation \JOO bi LAY shin\ (n.)
joy, celebration, exultation
Derek's **jubilation** over having his band beg him to come back was evident in his new song, *Me So Happy!*

justify \JUS tih fi\ (v.) -ied, -ing
to prove valid
Paul **justified** not helping his father clean out the garage by saying he had to volunteer at the Senior Center that afternoon.

juxtaposition \juks ta po ZISH un\ (n.)
side-by-side placement for comparison
Marisol looked at the **juxtaposition** of her photograph and her self-portrait, and realized they looked nothing alike.

kin \KIN\ (n.)
family, relatives
George had to admit that he loved the holidays; it was the only time he and his widespread **kin** got together.

larceny
\LAR suh nee\ (n.)
theft of property

Paul quickly dialed the police when he witnessed a man committing **larceny** by stealing a car.

latent \LAY tent\ (adj.)
present but hidden; potential

Ashley's **latent** aggravation began to emerge when she yelled at the other cheerleaders to stop socializing and start practicing.

lavish \LA vish\ (adj.)
extravagant, profuse

Josh felt as if he was going to burst after eating one portion of everything at the **lavish** dinner party his aunt was hosting.

ledger \LEJ er\ (n.)
a book that tracks finances

Shanna noticed in the student council **ledger** that some funds seemed to be missing and vowed to locate them by the end of the day.

legion \LEE jun\ (n.)
a great number,
a multitude
On Valentine's Day,
there was a **legion** of
boys waiting to give
Chantalle flowers when
she arrived in home-
room that morning.

lenient \LEEN yent\ (adj.)
easygoing, permissive
George felt the principal was too **lenient** when
he gave Willow a warning for cutting class,
since he always gave George detention for the
same offense.

liability \li uh BIL uh tee\ (n.)
handicap, something holding one back
Chantalle felt that sometimes, being beautiful
was a **liability** because it made guys feel
intimidated around her.

liberate \LIB uh rayt\ (v.) -ed, -ing
emancipate, set free
On Friday afternoon, the students were
liberated for the weekend by the sound of the
final bell.

linchpin \LINCH pin\ (n.)
central cohesive element
Paul's grandmother is the **linchpin** of the family.

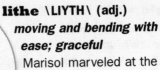

lithe \LIYTH\ (adj.)
moving and bending with ease; graceful
Marisol marveled at the **lithe** movements of the ballerina onstage at the ballet.

litigant \LIT ih gant\ (n.)
one involved in a lawsuit
George watched the **litigants** enter the courtroom on his favorite television show, *The People's Courtroom*.

loath \LOWTH\ (adj.)
reluctant, unwilling
Josh was **loath** to enter the coach's office because he knew he was in trouble for missing practice.

lobby \LOB bee\ (v.) -ed, -ing
to petition
Willow **lobbied** her congressman to stop the cigarette companies from advertising to teens.

longevity \lon JEV ih tee\ (n.)
long life
Timmy's ninety-eight-year-old grandfather says he owes his **longevity** to eating yogurt every day.

lubricate \LOOB rih kayt\ (v.) -ed, -ing
to grease up, make slippery
Timmy **lubricated** the joints on his robot so
that they would not squeak during the science
fair demonstration.

lull \LUL\ (v.)
to calm
George used white noise to **lull** himself to
sleep at night.

lummox \LUM iks\ (n.)
clumsy or stupid oaf
A bit of a **lummox**, Shanna avoids going into
stores displaying breakables because she
knows she's liable to knock something over.

lurid \LOO rid\ (adj.)
harshly shocking; sensational; glowing
Intrigued by the **lurid** headline in the tabloid,
Ashley quickly moved on to read the juicy
celebrity gossip.

lyricist \LIR ih sist\ (n.)
*person who writes words
for a song*
Timmy approached
Derek about being a
lyricist for Derek's band
by suggesting they put
Timmy's poetry to music.

M

machination
\mak uh NAY shun\ (n.)
crafty scheme; covert plot
Chantalle's **machinations** to attract the attention of her archenemy's newest boyfriend began with heavy-duty flirting whenever the girl wasn't around.

magnify \MAG nih fiy\ (v.) -ied, -ing
make greater in size, enlarge
Timmy really wanted to pop the zit on his chin, but he resisted, knowing it would only **magnify** the problem.

malediction \mal ih DIK shun\ (n.)
curse
Some students think cursing someone with the "evil eye" is a **malediction**; others think the evil eye is what Mrs. Bittman, the homeroom teacher, gives you if you come in late.

malinger \muh LING er\ (v.) -ed, -ing
to evade responsibility by pretending to be ill
George began **malingering** today so that tomorrow his mom would believe him when he said he was too sick to go to school.

mallet \MAL it\ (n.)
short-handled hammer
A **mallet**, which is a short-handed hammer, should not be confused with a mullet, which is an unfashionable haircut.

mandate \MAN dayt\ (n.)
a command or instruction
As the leader of the popular group, Chantalle felt she had a **mandate** to make fun of those whom she considered uncool.

manifest \MAN ih fest\ (adj.)
obvious
Shanna's mom thought their shopping trip was successful, but Shanna's disagreement became **manifest** when she never once wore the outfit they bought.

materialism \mu TEER ee uh lizm\ (n.)
preoccupation with worldly goods
As Chantalle sat in front of her plasma screen television talking on her new pda/cell phone, she couldn't understand why some people thought **materialism** was a bad thing.

matriarch \MAY tree ark\ (n.)
woman who rules family or clan
As the **matriarch**, Timmy's mom often makes decisions for the entire family.

maverick \MAV rik\ (n.)
one who breaks away from group conformity and forges a new course

As a rocker, Derek likes to consider himself a **maverick**, not realizing that he is simply part of the "rocker" clique, whose members look and act just like he does.

maxim \MAK sim\ (n.)
fundamental principle

Chantalle lives under the **maxim** "Do unto others before they do it to you."

meager \MEE grr\ (adj.)
minimal, scanty, deficient

George told the lunch lady to pile it on because there was no way he could get through the day on a **meager** portion of Sloppy Joe.

measured \ME zherd\ (adj.)
calculated, deliberate

The student took **measured** steps to improve his score on the SAT by studying vocabulary, grammar, and math.

mechanism \MEHK uh nizm\ (n.)
a machine or machine part

The "send" **mechanism** on Chantalle's two-way pager broke, leaving her unable to tell Shanna, who was in the next classroom, about her new pair of shoes.

meddler \MED ler\ (n.)
person interfering in others' affairs
Some people think that Willow is a **meddler** and should just mind her own business instead of trying to fix the world.

mediate \MEE dee ayt\
(v.) -ed, -ing
to resolve a dispute between two other parties
The referee **mediated** the disagreement on the soccer field.

meditate \MED ih tayt\
(v.) -ed, -ing
reflect on, contemplate
Sometimes Marisol **meditates** for weeks about her vision of a painting before she ever puts a brush to canvas.

medium \MEE dee um\ (n.)
psychic
After breaking up with her boyfriend, Willow decided to visit her favorite **medium** to find out if she would ever date again.

melee \MAY LAY\ (n.)
tumultuous free-for-all
Josh got suspended from school after starting a **melee** with the other team on the basketball court.

melodious \meh LOW dee us\ (adj.)
musical, pleasant to hear
Derek does his homework to the **melodious** sounds of the band "Burns Like Rubber."

mendicant \MEN dih kent\ (n.)
beggar
Josh felt a bit like a **mendicant** when he asked out the cute girl for the third time and she said she was busy . . . again.

merciless \MER sih less\ (adj.)
without pity
The Spanish teacher was notorious for his **merciless** pop quizzes, so his students were always prepared.

merriment \MER ree ment\ (n.)
high-spirited fun
The senior ski trip was full of **merriment**...until Shanna sprained her ankle.

methodical \me THOD ih kul\ (adj.)
systematic, orderly
The **methodical** way Timmy lined up his sixteen No. 2 pencils as he got ready to take his exam—one up, one down—was a little weird.

meticulous \meh TIK yoo luss\ (adj.)
extremely careful, fastidious, painstaking
Knowing that the diary on Shanna's desk was a fake one, Lisa's **meticulous** search led her to find the book that held her sister's real secrets.

miffed \MIFT\ (adj.)
offended, annoyed
Ashley was **miffed** when her boyfriend dumped her two days after she'd given him a birthday present.

milestone \MIYL stohn\ (n.)
important event in something or someone's history
Graduating high school is an important **milestone** in any student's life.

mimic \MIM ik\ (v.) -ked, -king
copy, imitate
Shanna complained to her mother because her little sister was **mimicking** everything she said.

mirage \mih RAZH\ (n.)
optical illusion, apparition
Timmy thought the pretty girl waving at him was a **mirage**, but she really did want to talk to him!

misconception \mis kon SEP shun\ (n.)
wrong understanding
It is a common **misconception** that all blondes are stupid.

missive \MIS iv\ (n.)
note or letter
George handed in the **missive** from his doctor
stating why he missed a week of school.

mitigate \MIT ih gayt\ (v.) -ed, -ing
to soften or make milder
Derek **mitigated** the tension between his band
members by treating them to pizza.

mock \MOK\ (v.) -ed, -ing
to deride, ridicule
The basketball team **mocked** Josh for
forgetting his sneakers and having to practice in
shorts, socks, and leather shoes.

moderate \MOD uh rit\
(adj.)
reasonable, not extreme
Chantalle might have
fibbed a little when she
told her mom that her
new handbag was
moderately priced.

modest \MOD est\ (adj.)
shy; plain, unassuming; moderate in size
Although she wished she could give more,
Willow made a **modest** donation to the Save
the Seals organization.

modicum \MOH di kum\ (n.)
small or token amount
Since the football players didn't even have a **modicum** of respect for the cheerleaders, Ashley, the head cheerleader, organized a boycott of the next football game.

modulate \MOJ uh layt\ (v.) -ed, -ing
to change pitch, intensity, or tone; to regulate
Derek **modulated** the tone of his guitar with a special effects pedal that was plugged into his speakers.

momentary \MOH men TE ree\ (adj.)
short-lived, lasting only for a short time
The **momentary** connection Willow and Derek felt in English class when they called out the same answer at the same time quickly passed, and by the end of the period they were back to disliking each other.

momentous \moh MEN tuss\ (adj.)
very important or significant
According to his mom, George choosing to clean his room rather than watch television was a **momentous** occasion—she never thought it would happen.

morality \mo RA li tee\ (n.)
concern for right and wrong
Willow's **morality** required her to always stand up for the underdog.

morass \mu RASS\ (n.)
marsh, an area of soggy ground
On a class trip, Chantalle lost a heel from her favorite pair of shoes in a grassy **morass**.

morose \mor ROHSS\ (adj.)
gloomy, sullen, or surly
Marisol was **morose** after receiving a rejection letter from her number one choice for college.

muddle \MUD il\ (v.) -ed, -ing
to jumble, to confuse; to bungle
Timmy tried to explain to the science fair judges how he had built his robot, but he was so nervous that he **muddled** the whole presentation.

mundane \mun DAYN\ (adj.)
ordinary, commonplace
The **mundane** lunchroom menu was spiced up one day by a visit from the chefs of a neighboring restaurant.

munificent \myoo NIF ih sint\ (adj.)
generous
The teacher **munificently** gave Willow a passing grade in gym even though she could not complete the three-mile run.

mutter \MUT er\ (v.) -ed, -ing
to grumble or complain
The class **muttered** and groaned when they were given a ton of physics homework.

mystify \MIST ih fiy\ (v.) -ied, -ing
to confuse or puzzle, to make obscure
George's parents were **mystified** when they heard him explaining the properties of calculus to a friend over the phone.

mythical \MITH ih kul\ (adj.)
fictitious element belonging to ancient stories
Most people believe that the unicorn is a **mythical** creature, but Willow suspects that unicorns really do exist.

naive \niy EEV\ (adj.)
lacking experience and understanding
Ashley had no idea how **naive** she would feel once she left her small town to attend college in a big city.

narcissism \NAR sih sizm\ (n.)
excessive love or admiration of oneself
Chantalle, the poster girl for **narcissism**, would not admit that she did, in fact, once have a pimple.

navigable \NAV ih guh bul\ (adj.)
sufficient for vessels to pass through
Although **navigable** for some, the choppy waters on the lake were too rough for a novice like Josh to sail safely.

nefarious \ni FAHR ee uss\ (adj.)
vicious, evil
Timmy debated whether or not his plan of revenge against Josh was actually too **nefarious** to implement.

negate \neh GAYT\ (v.) -ed, -ing
nullify, deny
Chantalle **negated** the rumor that she said
Shanna looked like a stuffed sausage in her jeans.

negligent \NEG lih jent\ (adj.)
careless, inattentive
Ashley was **negligent** in her duties as pep
squad captain when she forgot to order uniforms for the three new members.

negligible \NEG lih ju bul\ (adj.)
not worth considering
Chantalle wanted to go to a college near the
beach, but her parents refused because her
prospective colleges were all **negligible** party
schools.

neutrality \noo TRAL ih tee\ (n.)
disinterest, impartiality
Derek tried to emit a vibe of **neutrality** when,
in fact, he was psyched that his old girlfriend
wanted him back.

neutralize \NOO truh liyz\
(v.) -ed, -ing
to balance, offset
When Timmy cleaned his
fish tank, he added chemi-
cals to **neutralize** the chlo-
rine in the new water so that his
goldfish, Sparky, wouldn't keel over.

nonchalant \non shuh LAHNT\ (adj.)
calm, casual, seemingly unexcited
Paul acted **nonchalant** when he heard Marisol had broken up with her boyfriend, but inside he was totally excited.

nondescript \non des KRIPT\ (adj.)
lacking interesting or distinctive qualities
Marisol liked the fact that her prom dress made from old credit cards made a statement, unlike the **nondescript** black evening gowns everyone else was wearing.

nostalgic \nah STAHL jik\ (adj.)
longing for things of the past
After listening to his father's U2 CD, Paul began to feel **nostalgic** for the times he used to attend concerts with his dad.

notable \NO tu bul\ (adj.)
remarkable, worthy of notice
Josh's performance on the baseball field was so **notable** that scouts from colleges came to watch him play.

notion \NO shin\ (n.)
idea or conception
The **notion** that Willow would become a public advocate after college was well within the realm of possibility.

novelty \NOV ul tee\ (n.)
  something new and unusual
  At first George loved playing with his new video
  game unit, but soon the **novelty** wore off and
  he tossed it aside for something else.

novice \NAHV is\ (n.)
  beginner, apprentice
  Although Ashley is a
  novice bowler, she
  scored 102 when she
  went bowling Friday night
  with her friends.

nudge \NUJ\ (n.)
  gentle push
  Timmy told a corny joke. When his friend didn't
  laugh, Timmy **nudged** him in the ribs and asked
  if he understood the punch line.

nullify \NUL ih fi\ (v.) -ied, -ing
  *to make legally invalid; to counteract the
  effect of*
  The bar manager **nullified** his agreement to
  showcase Derek's band when he realized that the
  members of Snakebite were under twenty-one.

nurture \NUR chur\ (v.) -ed, -ing
  to help develop, cultivate
  After receiving a blue ribbon at the science fair,
  Timmy dedicated it to all the teachers who
  nurtured his curiosity for knowledge.

O

obdurate
\ AHB door it \ (adj.)
stubborn, hardhearted; inflexible
Josh was **obdurate** about living on campus when he started college; there was no way he would commute.

objective \ ob jek TIV \ (adj.)
impartial, uninfluenced by emotion
It was tough for Shanna to remain calm and **objective**, when the only person who could have divulged her embarrassing secret was her best friend.

oblivious \ ahb LIV ee us \ (adj.)
unaware, inattentive
Ashley walked around in a happy daze, totally **oblivious** that she was trailing toilet paper on her sneaker.

obnoxious \ ob NOK shiss \ (adj.)
objectionable, offensive
George's **obnoxious** belch at lunch confirmed to his girlfriend that he would never change.

obscure
\ahb SKYOOR\ (adj.)
not easily seen, inconspicuous
Timmy liked to study the life cycles of **obscure** insects for fun.

obsolete \ahb so LEET\ (adj.)
no longer in use; outdated
The invention of e-mail has made the concept of a handwritten letter almost **obsolete**.

obstacle \AHB stukl\ (n.)
impediment
Shanna never let her dyslexia become an **obstacle** to getting top grades.

obstinate \AHB stu nit\ (adj.)
stubborn
According to Chantalle, the **obstinate** woman continued to try on clothing from the Juniors department even after Chantalle was kind enough to tell her that she was too old to wear a belly shirt.

obstreperous \ahb STREP uh res\ (adj.)
troublesome, boisterous, unruly
Ashley decided that there were too many **obstreperous** kids running around the park that day for her to be able to study there in peace.

obtrusive \ahb TROO siv\ (adj.)
pushy, too conspicuous
Although it was a bit **obtrusive**, Shanna interrupted the teacher's conversation with the principal to ask him why she received only a B on her paper.

odometer \oh DOM ih ter\ (n.)
instrument in vehicles that indicates distance traveled
Josh tried driving in reverse to subtract the sixty miles from the **odometer** that he'd put on his father's sports car without consent.

onerous \OH ne rus\ (adj.)
burdensome
With nothing else to do one Sunday afternoon, Shanna took on the **onerous** task of organizing her cluttered closet.

onset \ON set\ (n.)
start
Ashley had lots of energy at the **onset** of the dance-a-thon, but by the twelfth hour she and her partner were totally exhausted.

opportune \ahp pur TOON\ (adj.)
appropriate, fitting
Paul finds that the **opportune** time to call his girlfriend is at 7:30 PM because it's late enough not to interrupt dinner and early enough not to annoy her parents.

optimistic \op tuh MIS tik\ (adj.)
expecting things to turn out well
The counselor wasn't sure why George was so **optimistic** about getting into Yale, since the boy was in danger of being held back.

opulence \AHP yu lens\ (n.)
wealth
Chantalle purchased the imitation designer purse because she wanted to ooze **opulence** without having to pay the price.

oration \aw RAY shun\ (n.)
lecture, formal speech
Shanna made sure her voice was loud and clear during her **oration** in front of the P.T.A.

orderly \OR der lee\ (adj.)
neat, systematic
Much to his mother's surprise, Josh had arranged his collection of college brochures into a neat and **orderly** stack on his desk.

originality \uh rij uh NAL ih tee\ (n.)
the ability to think independently
In an effort to prove her **originality**, Marisol shaved her head, knowing that no other girl in her class would have the guts to do it.

ornate \ohr NAYT\ (adj.)
elaborately ornamented
The **ornate** design on Chantalle's fingernails
seemed a little trashy to Ashley.

orthodox \OR thu doks\ (adj.)
adhering to what is customary or traditional
Derek's parents asked him to dress in an
orthodox fashion for his college interview;
that, of course, meant taking out the piercings
in his nose, ears, and left eyebrow.

ostensible \ah STEN sih bul\ (adj.)
apparent
The **ostensible** reason for Shanna studying so
hard is that she wants to get good grades; the real
reason is that she wants to please her parents.

ostentatious
\ah sten TAY shus\ (adj.)
showy
Willow thought the big dangly
earrings that Shanna wore to
school were gaudy and
ostentatious, but Chantalle
thought they were kind of cute.

ostracism \AHS tra sizm\ (n.)
exclusion, temporary banishment
Derek's **ostracism** from the dinner table last
night was rescinded when he apologized for
talking rudely to his parents.

outcast \OWT kast\ (n.)
someone rejected from a society
Timmy was tired of feeling like an **outcast**, so he introduced himself to some kids he didn't know at his lunch table.

outdated
\owt DAY tid\ (adj.)
old-fashioned, out of style
Although it was an **outdated** gesture, Ashley placed an apple on her favorite teacher's desk in a show of appreciation for his dedication.

overcome \oh ver KUM\ (v.) overcame, -ing
defeat, conquer
At the carnival, Willow **overcame** her fear of snakes and touched the one that was draped over the carnival lady's shoulders.

overpowering \oh ver POW er ing\ (adj.)
overwhelming
After his girlfriend made him watch four musicals in a row on TV, Josh had to fight the **overpowering** urge to burst into song and dance every time he wanted to make a point.

overshadow \oh ver SHA dow\ (v.) -ed, -ing
to obscure; to dominate
Although Paul was an excellent student, his trouble-making shenanigans **overshadowed** his grades.

pallid \PAL id\ (adj.)
lacking color or liveliness
George's **pallid** complexion was due to the fact that he was a couch potato who spent most of his free time in front of the TV.

pantomime \pan toh MIYM\ (n.)
communication through gestures
Marisol thought it would be a fun experiment to spend a day communicating through **pantomime** rather than talking to people.

paradox \PAR uh doks\ (n.)
contradiction, incongruity; dilemma, puzzle
It's a sad **pardox** that so many girls assume they need to diet to be beautiful when lots of guys are attacted to girls with curves.

paramount \PAR uh mownt\ (adj.)
supreme, dominant, primary
Ashley believed it was of **paramount** importance to develop social skills in high school, so that when she went away to college it would be easy to make new friends.

142

paranoid \PAR uh noyd\ (adj.)
exhibiting extreme mistrust
After accidentally walking underneath a ladder, Paul became **paranoid** that something awful was going to happen to him that day.

paraphrase \PAR uh frayz\ (v.) -ed, -ing
to reword, usually in simpler terms
Some students believe that it's not plagiarism if you **paraphrase** a section from a book to use in a school paper, but technically, it is.

parasite \PAR uh siyt\ (n.)
person or animal that lives at another's expense
Chantalle was disgusted as she watched her **parasite** of a date shove large handfuls of her popcorn into his mouth at the movies after he'd refused to buy his own.

parched \PARCH t\ (adj.)
dried up, shriveled
Chantalle's date was **parched** after eating all of Chantalle's popcorn during the movie, so he took a big swig of her soda.

pariah \puh RIY uh\ (n.)
outcast
The number one **pariah** at the high school was a sophomore who openly picked his nose and ate it in front of other students.

parity \PAR ih tee\ (n.)
  equality
  Although her parents maintained **parity** between Shanna and her sister, Shanna believed that Lisa received preferential treatment.

partisan \PAR ti zun\ (n.)
  strong supporter
  Willow is known as a **partisan** of almost every cause that protects the environment.

passive \PASS iv\ (adj.)
  submissive; inactive
  Chantalle cut in front of a group of **passive**-looking boys on line at the music store. Sure enough, instead of getting angry, they just smiled and let her in the line.

pathetic \puh THET ik\ (adj.)
  arousing scornful pity
  Timmy held in his laughter when he saw Josh's **pathetic** excuse for an algorithm on the chalkboard.

pathos \PAY thohs\ (n.)
  pity, compassion
  Shanna loved Shakespeare's plays because they contained both comedy and **pathos**.

peer \PEER\ (n.)
  contemporary, equal, match
  Ashley approached a group of her **peers** with a big smile and asked them if they were going to attend the school dance on Saturday.

penitent \PEN ih tent\ (adj.)
expressing sorrow for sins or offenses, repentant
George was **penitent** for toilet-papering the principal's front yard only after he got caught.

penurious \peh NOOR ee us\ (adj.)
stingy; poverty-stricken
Marisol swore that she would rather live a **penurious** life and be free to create art than get a lucrative, corporate job that would stifle her creative genius.

perception \per SEP shun\ (n.)
act or ability to see or understand
The students' **perception** of what was cool and what wasn't was often determined by the opinions of their peers.

perfidious \pir FID ee uss\ (adj.)
faithless, disloyal, untrustworthy
Timmy was incensed when his **perfidious** friends told Josh that Timmy's favorite movie is *The Wizard of Oz*.

perfunctory
\pir FUNK tu ree\ (adj.)
indifferent; done in a routine manner
George's **perfunctory** attitude toward personal hygiene habits often gets him into trouble with the people around him.

periodic \pir ee ODD ik\ (adj.)
recurring from time to time; cyclical
Ashley **periodically** practiced different smiles
in the mirror just in case someone wanted to
spontaneously take her picture.

perjure \PIR joor\ (v.) -ed, -ing
to tell a lie under oath
Paul **perjured** himself when
he swore on his dead gerbil
that he returned the overdue
DVD to the video store, when
it was still in his backpack.

perplex \pir PLEKS\ (v.) -ed, -ing
to confuse
Josh's explanation of a ground-rule double during
the high school baseball game **perplexed** Ashley.
She had no idea what he was talking about.

persevere \pir suh VEER\ (v.) -ed, -ing
to refuse to stop no matter how hard something is
Willow decided to **persevere** with her yoga
practice until she could twist herself into a
pretzel shape.

persistence \pir SIS tuns\ (n.)
the act, state, or quality of not giving up
Although the task was tough, Ashley's
persistence paid off when she convinced four
hundred students to cheer for their home team
at the girls' varsity swim meet.

perspicacious \pur spi KAY shuss\ (adj.)
shrewd, astute, keen-witted
The **perspicacious** teacher knew that George was not paying attention in class, so she called on him to answer a question.

pertinent \PIR tih nent\ (adj.)
applicable, appropriate
Paul used index cards to make sure he included all the **pertinent** information in his oral report on the Civil War.

pervasive \pir VAY siv\ (adj.)
tending to pervade, spreading throughout
The delicious smell of cinnamon buns was so **pervasive** throughout the mall that Marisol felt compelled to go to the food court to buy one.

pessimism \PES uh mizm\ (n.)
negativity
No one could accuse Ashley of **pessimism** as she always looks on the bright side of things.

phlegmatic \fleg MAT ik\ (adj.)
calm in temperament; sluggish
George's **phlegmatic** work ethic was evident when he took four hours to stack a pile of sweaters for his boss.

pigment \PIG ment\ (n.)
substance used for coloring
Marisol created a gorgeous shade of green by mixing yellow and blue **pigments** into her white paint.

placate \PLAY kayt\ (v.) -ed, -ing
to soothe or pacify
After accidentally dumping a chili dog onto her skirt, Josh tried to **placate** Chantalle by offering to pay for her dry cleaning.

placebo \plu SEE boh\ (n.)
a substance with no medical value that is given as medication
Shanna's sister, Lisa, said she felt much smarter after swallowing one of Shanna's coveted "smart pills." She had no idea that it was a **placebo**; Shanna had given her a bottle of TicTacs.

plagiarize \PLAY ju riyz\ (v.) -ed, -ing
to pass off another's ideas as one's own
George got an F on a paper when the teacher realized that he'd **plagiarized** another student's work.

plaudits \PLAW ditz\ (n.)
enthusiastic praise
Marisol received **plaudits** from her art teacher when she displayed her magnificent rendering of the van Gogh painting *Starry Night*.

plentiful \PLEN tih ful\ (adj.)
abundant
Josh was psyched to find a **plentiful** supply of pigs in a blanket, his favorite snack, on a tray in the fridge.

ploy \PLOY\ (n.)
maneuver, plan
George's **ploy** to butter up his teacher so that she'd forget about all the missing homework and give him an A was unsuccessful.

polarize \POH lu ryz\ (v.) -ed, -ing
to tend toward opposite extremes
The school was **polarized** over the issue of pass/fail grading. Half the students thought it was a great idea; the other half thought it would ruin their chances of getting into good colleges.

pomp \POMP\ (n.)
dignified display, splendor
Ashley waved graciously as she accepted her title and took in the **pomp** of the Miss Apple Pie crowning ceremony in the town square.

pompous \POM pus\ (adj.)
pretentious
Chantalle wondered if admitting how glad she was to be so beautiful and talented was a bit **pompous**, even if it was totally true.

postpone \post POHN\ (v.) -ed, -ing
defer, delay
Shanna **postponed** her date for an hour so that she could get her hair just right.

potentate \POH tn tayt\ (n.)
monarch or ruler with great power
Shanna tried to explain to Chantalle that she's class president, not a **potentate**, and therefore can't convince the principal to turn the cafeteria into a coffeehouse.

pragmatic \prag MAT ik\ (adj.)
practical; moved by facts rather than abstract ideals
Timmy's **pragmatic** approach to learning how to play the mandolin was to practice for at least one hour every day.

prank \PRANK\ (n.)
practical joke
Paul promised his mom that he'd stop playing **pranks** on the kids at school, which meant he'd have to leave the rubber tarantula at home.

preamble \PRE am bul\ (n.)
introductory passage
The **preamble** to the student bylaws was so boring that Derek skipped right over it. All he wanted to know was whether his favorite death metal T-shirt would violate the dress code.

precedent \PRESS uh dent\ (n.)
earlier example of a similar situation
Josh's older brother set a **precedent** for athletic achievement in their family by scoring the most points ever in a high school basketball game.

precept \PREE sept\ (n.)
principle; law
Timmy chucked his pocket protector, his calculator, and his nerdy sweater into the trash when he realized that there was no **precept** that states geniuses had to dress like dorks.

precious \PRESH us\ (adj.)
valuable; beloved
Willow couldn't resist the **precious** little puppy at the pound so she took the puppy home and asked her parents if she could keep it.

precipitate \pri SIP ih tit\ (adj.)
sudden and unexpected; reckless
Paul's **precipitate** decision to jump out from around a corner and scare Shanna seemed to cure her of her hiccups once and for all.

preclude \pre KLOOD\
(v.) -ed, -ing
prevent, exclude
Ashley was **precluded** from cheering at the big game because she forgot to wear her uniform.

precocious \pri KOH shiss\ (adj.)
unusually advanced or talented at an early age
Lisa, Shanna's **precocious** little sister, has developed advanced blackmailing skills, thanks to years of practicing on Shanna.

predetermine \pree deh TER min\ (v.) -ed, -ing
to decide in advance
Timmy had **predetermined** that he would show the mysterious scar on his stomach only to people who believed him when he said he was abducted by aliens. So far, no one had seen it.

predictable \pre DIKT uh bul\ (adj.)
expected beforehand
Timmy's weekend routine was always so **predictable**; every Saturday night he played mini-golf with his friends at the Putt Hut.

predominant \pre DOM ih nunt\ (adj.)
most important or conspicuous
Although the **predominant** feature on Marisol's face was her rather large nose, she would never think of getting plastic surgery.

prepossessing \pree pu ZES ing\ (adj.)
attractive, engaging, appealing
Josh thought that Chantalle was the most **prepossessing** right after she had exercised in gym class and had a healthy glow on her face.

preserve \pre ZURV\ (v.) -ed, -ing
to protect, to keep unchanged
Timmy slathers on sunscreen every morning because he wants to **preserve** his youthful appearance as long as possible.

pretense \PRE tenss\ (n.)
false appearance or action
Shanna entered the furrier's shop under the
pretense of shopping for a pink chinchilla
jacket but she just wanted to try on a few furs,
not actually buy one.

pretentious \pri TEN shuss\ (adj.)
*pretending to be important, intelligent,
or cultured*
Derek laughed as Chantalle entered the music
club, acting all snobby and **pretentious**, because
it was clear to him that she was just a poser.

primary \PRY meh ree\ (adj.)
main; first; earliest
The **primary** reason that Shanna won the election for class president is that she is popular.
The secondary reason is that she's smart.

proclaim \pro KLAYM\ (v.) -ed, -ing
announce officially
Timmy wanted to approach the girl who worked
at the coffeehouse and **proclaim** that he liked
her, but he kept chickening out.

procrastinate \pro KRAS tih nayt\ (v.) -ed, -ing
to put off doing work
Rather than study for finals, Shanna
procrastinated by taking her little sister to the
park for an hour.

procure \pro KYOOR\ (v.) -ed, -ing
to acquire, obtain; to get
Marisol showed her friend the new acrylic paints that she had **procured** at the art store; they were so pretty that she didn't want to use them up.

prod \PRAHD\ (v.) -ed, -ing
poke, nudge, in the literal and figurative sense
Derek's friends **prodded** him to graffiti the handball wall at the high school, but in the end, he just couldn't do it.

prodigy \PRAHD ih jee\ (n.)
person with exceptional talents
When Josh was two years old his parents thought he was a **prodigy** because he could count from one to ten in Spanish. Unfortunately his Spanish skills have not improved since.

profane \pro FAYN\ (adj.)
impure; contrary to religion; sacrilegious
Timmy's mom heard him utter some **profane** comments about Josh and made him wash his mouth out with soap.

profound \pro FOWND\ (adj.)
deep, meaningful; far-reaching
Paul's determination to improve his writing skills had a **profound** effect on his college applications.

profusion \ pro FYOO zhin \ (n.)
abundance, extravagance
The walls of Marisol's room were covered with a **profusion** of images: posters, photos, magazine covers, and her own paintings and sketches.

prohibit \pro HIB it\ (v.) -ed, -ing
to forbid, prevent
Shanna's parents **prohibited** her from dating older boys, but that didn't stop her from doing so.

proliferate \pro LIF uh rayt\ (v.) -ed, -ing
propagate, reproduce; enlarge, expand
Ashley's idea of dressing in the school colors every Monday **proliferated** throughout the school and soon everyone was doing it.

prolific \pro LIF ik\ (adj.)
productive, fertile
Marisol was a **prolific** artist, who had so far produced two hundred and forty-seven paintings.

prominence \PROM ih nence\ (n.)
importance, eminence
Shanna will be given great **prominence** at graduation because she had the highest grade point average in the senior class.

promote \pru MOHT\ (v.) -ed, -ing
to contribute to the progress of
Willow did her best to **promote** the clothing drive at school by hanging random pieces of clothing from people's lockers to remind them.

promulgate \PROM ul gayt\ (v.) -ed, -ing
to make known publicly
When the school board **promulgated** their new, more-difficult testing standards, George knew he was in big trouble.

propagate \PROP uh gayt\ (v.) -ed, -ing
to spread out; to have offspring
The rumor about Chantalle sending herself roses for Valentine's Day **propagated** around school in a flash.

propel \pro PEL\ (v.) -ed, -ing
to cause to move forward
Timmy watched in awe as the cannon in the main ring of the circus fired and **propelled** the man to the other side of the tent.

prophetic \pro FET ik\ (adj.)
foretelling events by divine means
Derek's horoscope about having a hot date this weekend proved **prophetic** when his ex asked him out.

proponent \pruh POH nent\ (n.)
advocate, defender, supporter
Ashley was a strong **proponent** of treating others the way she wanted to be treated.

propriety \pro PRY ih tee\ (n.)
correct behavior; appropriateness
Since George did not have a tissue, **propriety**
demanded that he wait until he found one to
blow his nose, when all he wanted to do was
wipe his nose on his sleeve.

prosaic \pro ZAY ik\ (adj.)
relating to prose; dull, commonplace
Josh gave a **prosaic** speech in his American history class that made even the teacher doze off.

prospect \PROSS pekt\ (n.)
possibility, chance
Shanna's college counselor told her that the
prospect of attaining a scholarship to her
first-choice college was very real.

prosperity \pross PER ih tee\ (n.)
wealth or success
Timmy hoped he'd attain
prosperity in adulthood by inventing an automatic toilet paper dispenser and selling it to
millions of people.

protagonist \pro TAG uh nist\ (n.)
main character in a play or story; hero
Marisol often fantasized about dating an author
who would one day immortalize her as the
protagonist in his Pulitzer Prize-winning
spy novel.

protégé \PRO tuh zhay\ (n.)
one receiving personal direction and care from a mentor
Josh took on a **protégé** from the JV football team and taught him the throwing techniques that Josh had learned playing varsity.

prototype \PRO to tiyp\ (n.)
early, typical example
Finally, Timmy was ready to test the **prototype** of his automatic toilet paper dispenser.

provocative \proh VOK uh tiv\ (adj.)
tending to provoke a response, usually anger or disagreement
The history teacher began the class with a **provocative** statement about World War II in order to begin a debate in class.

proximity \prok SIM ih tee\ (n.)
nearness
Shanna was bummed when a blue car grabbed the only parking spot in **proximity** to her favorite store. Now she'd have to park on the other side of the mall.

prudent \PROOD int\ (adj.)
careful, cautious
Willow felt it **prudent** to walk the long way home rather than take a shortcut by crossing the highway.

prune \PROON\ (v.) -ed, -ing
to trim dead parts of a branch
Paul helped his mother with the gardening by
pruning the bushes in the backyard.

pun \PUN\ (n.)
play on words
Paul thought the **pun** he made about homework
was funny, but everyone else thought it was
just corny.

punctual \PUNK shoo ull\ (adj.)
on time
Since Willow is a **punctual** person, she thinks it
is rude when someone arrives late to an event.

pundit \PUN dit\ (n.)
critic; learned person
For his report on the Vietnam War, Paul inter-
viewed his uncle who was a **pundit** on the topic.

punitive \PYOO nih tiv\ (adj.)
having to do with punishment
Josh received **punitive** action by the referee
when he pushed a player on the opposing
baseball team.

pursuit \pur SOOT\ (n.)
the act of chasing or striving
George likes watching movies that end up with
the good guy in hot **pursuit** of the bad guy,
usually in the form of an exciting car chase.

quaint
\KWAYNT\ (adj.)
charmingly strange
Chantalle thought the accessories store on Main Street was **quaint** in comparison to the sprawling mall where she usually shopped.

quandary \KWAN du ree\ (n.)
predicament, dilemma
Derek was in a **quandary** when his band was called onstage for an encore—should they play, *Wag the Puppy* or *Scorpion Blood*?

quell \KWELL\ (v.) -ed, -ing
to pacify, to suppress
There was nothing Ashley could do to **quell** the arguing of the two girls who fought over the last brownie at the bake sale.

querulous \KWER uh lus\ (adj.)
complaining, grumbling
The principal, tired of the **querulous** attitude of the students, suspended the call for school uniforms.

query\ KWEH ree \ (v.) -ied, -ing
  to question
  Timmy **queried** Derek about how to get girls to like him, and Derek told him to learn how to play the guitar.

quip \KWIP\ (n.)
  clever, witty joke
  Paul thought his **quip** about the teacher's hairstyle was pretty funny until the teacher told him to go to the principal's office.

quizzical \KWIZ ih kul\ (adj.) *questioning*
  Timmy gave Derek a **quizzical** look when Derek said that girls would like him if he played the guitar, but two seconds later Timmy went off in search of the guitar teacher at school.

R

radiant \RAY dee unt\
(adj.)
glowing, beaming; emitting heat
Marisol looked **radiant** as she
walked the catwalk at the school fashion show, wearing a patchwork gown that
she had designed herself.

radical \RAD ih kul\ (adj.)
extreme, marked departure from the norm
Ashley tried to tell Willow, in a nice way, that
her boycott of deodorant was a **radical** assault
on everyone's right to breathe fresh air.

rail \RAYL\ (v.) -ed, -ing
to scold with bitter or abusive language
Josh laughed when he caught the coach **railing**
at an imaginary football ref in the mirror.

ramble \RAM bl\ (v.) -ed, -ing
to roam, wander; to babble, digress
Timmy **rambled** aimlessly through the mall
looking for his date, who had told him she'd be
right back—two hours ago.

rancorous \RANK o russ\ (adj.)
bitter, hateful
A **rancorous** argument erupted between the coach and the referee after a close call.

rascal \RAS kul\ (n.)
playful, mischievous person; a scoundrel
Although George was a **rascal** at times, the principal still liked the boy.

raspy \RAS pee\ (adj.)
rough, grating
Ashley's high-pitched voice turned low and **raspy** when she contracted bronchitis.

raucous \RAW kus\ (adj.)
harsh sounding; boisterous
The **raucous** senior carnival caused so much damage to the school's football field that the principal vowed never to host a carnival again.

raze \RAYZ\ (v.) -ed, -ing
to tear down, demolish
Once Timmy was rich and famous, he planned to **raze** his parents' weathered house and build a brand-new one in its place.

reactionary \re AK shun eh ree\ (adj.)
marked by extreme conservatism,
especially in politics
It's surprising how Willow is such a liberal
activist when her parents are known around
town as political **reactionaries**.

reap \REEP\ (v.) -ed, -ing
to obtain a return, often a harvest
Ashley **reaped** a reward of
twenty bucks after she found a
wallet and returned it to an
extremely grateful man.

rebate \REE bayt\ (n.)
deduction in amount to be paid
Paul received a 30 percent **rebate** on the new
stereo that he bought with the birthday money
his grandparents gave him.

rebuff \re BUFF\ (v.) -ed, -ing
to bluntly reject
Ashley **rebuffed** her classmate's offer to go on
a date that night because she thought it was
rude for a guy to ask a girl out at the last
minute.

recall \re KAWL\ (v.) -ed, -ing
remember; cancel, revoke; take back
Marisol sold some original purses that she'd
designed, then **recalled** them due to a
defective clasp.

reckless \REK lis\ (adj.)
careless, rash
Even though he was just imitating his favorite band, Derek's **reckless** behavior onstage at the school rock concert cost him a week of detention.

reconciliation \reh con sil ee AY shun\ (n.)
the resolution of a dispute
Sometimes Chantalle picked small fights with Shanna because their **reconciliations**—which always involved getting pedicures together— were so much fun.

recrimination \ree kri mi NAY shun\ (n.)
counter accusation
When Willow said that Marisol lacked any real artistic talent, Marisol retorted with the **recrimination** that Willow was a weirdo who lacked personality.

redundancy \ri DUN din see\ (n.)
unnecessary repetition
Josh handed in a five-page report on the intricacies of fly-fishing, but after his teacher marked all of the **redundancies**, he ended up with only two paragraphs of actual content.

refinement \ri FIYN ment\ (n.)
improvement, elegance
Although Chantalle was dressed beautifully for dinner, she showed her lack of **refinement** by chewing her food like a cow.

refracted \ri FRAK tid\ (adj.)
deflected, sharply bent
Marisol loved it when the **refracted** rays of sunlight made the clouds look bright pink, but she could never capture that exact color in her paintings.

refurbish \re FUR bish\ (v.) -ed, -ing
to renovate
Paul helped his father **refurbish** his mother's old coffee table and made it look brand-new.

refute \re FYOOT\ (v.) -ed, -ing
to contradict, discredit
Determined to **refute** the idea that she was totally spoiled, Chantalle decided to make dinner for her family, but when she couldn't find the take-out menus she suggested they go out to eat instead.

regale \re GAYL\ (v.) -ed, -ing
amuse, entertain
Timmy **regaled** the other people in the *Star Wars* chat room with tales of how he scared a telemarketer by speaking in his "Darth Vader" voice.

regurgitate \re GUR juh tayt\ (v.) -ed, -ing
rush, surge, or throw back
Most teachers prefer that their students
truly understand a subject rather than just
regurgitate a bunch of memorized facts
back to them.

rehash \re HASH\ (v.) -ed, -ing
bring forth again with no real change
When their mother asked what the problem
was, Shanna and Lisa **rehashed** their
argument for her.

reiterate \re IT uh rayt\ (v.) -ed, -ing
to say or do again, repeat
The coach **reiterated** the importance of the big
football game the next day because he wanted
to make sure that players understood the con-
sequences of losing.

relapse \ree LAPS\ (n.)
regress, backslide
Paul thought he had recov-
ered from the flu after resting for a week, but suffered
a **relapse** and got sick again.

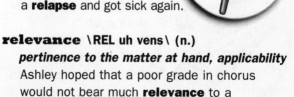

relevance \REL uh vens\ (n.)
pertinence to the matter at hand, applicability
Ashley hoped that a poor grade in chorus
would not bear much **relevance** to a
college acceptance.

relinquish \re LIN kwish\ (v.) -ed, -ing
to renounce or surrender something
Chantalle did not willingly **relinquish** the
alligator shoes at the sale; another girl yanked
them out of her hands and rushed to the cash
register to buy them.

relish \REH lish\ (v.) -ed, -ing
to enjoy greatly
George **relished** the tasty hot dog, which was
piled high with all the fixins.

reluctant \re LUK tant\ (adj.)
unwilling, opposing; hesitant
Derek was **reluctant** to shave off his Mohawk,
but his mother thought a clean-cut look would
impress college admissions officers.

rely \re LIY\ (v.) -ed, -ing
be dependant, have confidence
Shanna knows that she can **rely** on the good
study habits she formed in high school to get
her through college successfully.

remiss \ri MISS\ (adj.)
*negligent or carelessness
about a job*
Timmy was **remiss** in his
job in the principal's
office and accidentally sta-
pled a teacher's memo to
his math homework.

remnant \REM nent\ (n.)
something left over, surviving trace
George saw nothing wrong with the fact that he was eating the **remnants** of his potato chips that had spilled onto the living room carpet the day before.

remorseful \re MORS ful\ (adj.)
feeling sorry for sins
Marisol felt **remorseful** for accidentally dripping some paint onto her mother's new couch.

remote \re MOHT\ (adj.)
distant, isolated
Paul knew there wasn't even a **remote** chance that Marisol would go out with him that weekend, so he didn't bother asking her.

remuneration \ri myoon eh RAY shun\ (n.)
pay or reward for work, trouble, etc.
The old lady offered to pay Paul for helping with her groceries, but he told her that a piece of her home-made blueberry pie was all the **remuneration** he needed.

renovation \ren oh VAY shun\ (n.)
repair, making something new again
The school's dingy old gym was in need of some major **renovation**.

renunciation \re nun see AY shin\ (n.) *rejection of beliefs*

It was clear that Shanna's sudden **renunciation** of horror flicks was due to the nightmares she had after watching *Living Corpse 5*.

repel \re PEL\ (v.) -led, -ling
to rebuff, repulse; disgust, offend

The idea of smoking cigarettes **repelled** Ashley because she thought that cigarettes made people smell bad.

repentant \re PEN tent\ (adj.)
apologetic, remorseful, guilty

George was particularly **repentant** for sneaking a bite of dip from his friend's kitchen when he realized that the dip was actually cat food.

replicate \REP lih kayt\ (v.) -ed, -ing
to duplicate, repeat

According to Marisol, the good thing about abstract art is that you can never **replicate** the same piece twice.

repress \re PRESS\ (v.) -ed, -ing
to restrain or hold in

Chantalle **repressed** the urge to check her e-mail for new messages because she had just checked it five minutes ago.

reprieve \re PREEV\ (n.)
postponement of a punishment; relief from danger
Shanna was given a **reprieve** from her loss of
phone privileges so that she could call her
grandmother on her birthday.

reprimand \REP rih mand\ (v.) -ed, -ing
rebuke, admonish
Willow **reprimanded** her puppy for having an
"accident" in the kitchen, and then cleaned it
up before her parents could notice.

repudiate \re PYOO dee ayt\ (v.) -ed, -ing
to reject as having no authority
Josh's offhand comment that he ran the football team was **repudiated** when the coach gave
him fifty push-ups for being late to practice.

reputable \REH pyoo tu bul\ (adj.)
honorable, respectable
Shanna heard from a very **reputable** source
that she was going to be voted Prom Queen.

requisition
\re kwi ZIH shun\
(v.) -ed, -ing
to demand the use of
Josh **requisitioned** the
freshman's No. 2 pencil
in the library, and the kid
quickly handed it over.

reserve \re ZERV\ (n.)
something put aside for future use
Chantalle put her favorite movie, *Breakfast in the Hamptons,* on **reserve** at the video store because she intended to rent it over the weekend.

resilient \re ZIL yent\ (adj.)
quick to recover, bounce back
Although Marisol was mortified when a button on her shirt popped off during the opening act of the school play, she was **resilient** enough to hold it together and finish the scene.

resolute \REZ uh loot\ (adj.)
determined; with a clear purpose
Derek was **resolute** that he'd never stop creating music even if he never became a famous rock star.

resource \REE sors\ (n.)
something that can be used
Willow wanted to buy some birdseed to feed the pigeons in the park, but she did not have the financial **resources** to do so.

resplendent \ri SPLEN dent\ (adj.)
splendid, brilliant, dazzling
Paul told his date that her eyes looked **resplendent** in the light of the silvery moon because he thought she would think it was romantic. Instead, she burst out laughing.

restore \reh STOR\ (v.) -ed, -ing
reestablish; revive
In an effort to **restore** his abs to the six-pack he once had, Josh began a regimen of two hundred sit-ups a day.

restrained \ri STRAY nd\ (adj.)
controlled, repressed, restricted
Shanna took a **restrained** breath before she told her parents that she, um, kind of lost their car in the mall's parking lot.

retain \ri TAYN\ (v.) -ed, -ing
to hold, keep possession of
Ashley was surprised to learn that her mother had **retained** the memory of every Mother's Day since Ashley was born.

retract \re TRAKT\ (v.) -ed, -ing
to take back or draw in
Josh **retracted** his statement that Rollerblading® was "so easy" when he tried it and fell down multiple times.

retroactive \ret roh AK tiv\ (adj.)
applying to an earlier time
Willow was psyched that her raise at the Tofu Barn was **retroactive**, which meant that not only would she get paid more this month, but she would get extra money for working last month, too.

revelry \REV ul ree\ (n.)
boisterous festivity

The student body burst into **revelry** when a power outage caused the school day to end early.

revere \ri VEER\ (v.) -ed, -ing
to worship, regard with awe
Timmy thought all of his hard work was worth it when he was **revered** by the other players at the National Teen Chess Masters tournament.

revive \reh VIYV\ (v.) -ed, -ing
resuscitate, bring back to life; restore to use
When Ashley is feeling blah, she likes to **revive** herself with a peppermint-toffee swirl ice cream cone.

revoke \ri VOHK\ (v.) -ed, -ing
to annul, cancel, call back
Paul's public library card was **revoked** because he forgot to return some books he had borrowed back in second grade.

rhapsody \RAP su dee\ (n.)
emotional literary or musical work
Derek wrote a beautiful **rhapsody** about his first day in kindergarten that he would never, ever perform in public.

rhetorical \ri TOR ih kul\ (adj.)
related to using language effectively
"Do you think I'm stupid or something?" is generally a **rhetorical** question. If asked this question, do not feel the need to answer "yes."

roster \ROS ter\ (n.)
a list of names
Josh's name appears at the top of the high school football **roster** because he is the team captain.

rouse \ROWZ\ (v.) -ed, -ing
provoke, excite, stir
Ashley's job as head cheerleader is to **rouse** the fans and to cheer on the home team.

rude \ROOD\ (adj.)
crude, primitive, uncouth
Willow found George's sloppy eating habits **rude**, yet strangely captivating.

ruthless \ROOTH less\ (adj.)
merciless, compassionless
The AP American History teacher was infamous for giving **ruthless** exams.

sacrosanct
\SAK roh sangkt\ (adj.)
sacred

Chantalle considered her New York City snow globe **sacrosanct** and wouldn't let even her best friend touch it.

safeguard \SAYF gard\ (n.)
precautionary measure

Josh asked his buddy to spot him in the weight room as a **safeguard** in case he couldn't handle the weights by himself.

sagacious \su GAY shiss\ (adj.)
wise, shrewd

Willow will always remember Mr. Balaban as the **sagacious** English teacher who introduced her to the writings of J.R.R. Tolkien.

salvage \SAL vij\ (v.) -ed, -ing
to recover, save from loss

In an effort to **salvage** his chance of graduating on time, George tried to attend all his classes.

sanctimonious \sangk ti MOH nee us\ (adj.)
excessive righteousness
Students in the lunchroom were starting to get
tired of Willow's **sanctimonious** speeches
about the perils of eating red meat.

scamper \SKAM per\ (v.) -ed, -ing
run off quickly
Willow hurried to keep up as her puppy
scampered down the path in the park.

scapegoat \SKAYP goht\ (n.)
someone blamed for every problem
Paul accidentally spilled a
glass of cranberry juice on
the living room rug and
used his dog, Muffin, as
a **scapegoat** by saying
that Muffin had knocked
over the glass.

scholarly \SKOL ur lee\ (adj.)
related to higher learning
Timmy was looking forward to leaving boring
high school classes behind in favor of more
scholarly pursuits.

scorn \SKORN\ (n.)
contempt, derision
Josh's teammates regarded him with **scorn**
when he drank all the Gatorade the team had
planned to dump over the coach's head.

scoundrel \SKOWN drul\ (n.)
villain, rogue
To Timmy, Josh is a bully and a **scoundrel** but to Ashley, Josh is a total hottie.

scour \SKOWER\ (v.) -ed, -ing
to scrub clean
Marisol had to **scour** her paint-stained fingernails with a whole bar of soap before she could get them clean.

scrupulous \SKROOP yu luss\ (adj.)
restrained; honest; careful and precise
Ashley has such a **scrupulous** nature that she once chased down a girl for three blocks in order to return a bracelet the girl had dropped on the street instead of keeping it for herself.

scrutinize \SKROO tin iyz\ (v.) -ed, -ing
to observe carefully
Paul **scrutinized** the three hairs growing on his chin, wondering if he should shave them.

scurry \SKUR ree\
(v.) -ied, -ing
scamper, run lightly
Marisol screamed when she spotted a mouse **scurrying** across the tiles in the girls' bathroom at school.

secrete \se KREET\ (v.) -ed, -ing
to release fluids from a body
Timmy took a sample of the weird pus **secreting** from the scab on his knee, and checked it out under his microscope.

sedative \SED uh tiv\ (n.)
something that calms or soothes
Willow uses ginger tea as a **sedative** for her stomach when it feels upset.

sequel \SEE kwul\ (n.)
literary or artistic work that continues a previous piece
George loved the action movie so much that he hoped the producer would make a **sequel** to continue the story.

serendipity \se ren DIP ih tee\ (n.)
habit of making fortunate discoveries by chance
Marisol thought it was **serendipity** that she tripped over that backpack in the hallway at school; the owner of the backpack later became her boyfriend.

serene \se REEN\ (adj.)
calm; peaceful
Willow took a moment to enjoy the atmosphere of the **serene** beach during sunset.

servile \SUR viyl\ (adj.)
overly submissive
Chantalle's boyfriend of the week was quite **servile** and catered to her every whim.

setback \SET back\ (n.)
change from better to worse
Ashley's pizza party had a minor **setback**
when the pizzas delivered had anchovies on
them, when Ashley had specifically requested
mushrooms only.

severe \se VEER\ (adj.)
*harsh, strict, extremely bad
in degree*
The group thought it would be
fun to explore the haunted
house, except for Ashley, who
stayed outside with a **severe**
case of the heebie-jeebies.

shabby \SHA bee\ (adj.)
worn-out, threadbare, deteriorated
Marisol didn't think her clothes looked that
shabby until Chantalle asked her if she
shopped in a Dumpster.

shroud \SHROWD\ (v.) -ed, -ing
to conceal or hide
Willow **shrouded** her Tarot cards with a silk
cloth so that their energy could not escape.

shun \SHUN\ (v.) -ned, -ning
avoid deliberately
Derek **shunned** Willow's personal Web page
because he knew she had written a blog about
how unoriginal she thought his band was.

signpost \SIYN post\ (n.)
indication, guide
Derek didn't know exactly what career he would pursue if he didn't become a rock star, but all the **signposts** indicated that he would be working in the music industry.

skepticism \SKEP tih sizm\ (n.)
doubt, disbelief; uncertainty
Despite Josh's **skepticism**, his dad proved that he could get tickets to the Super Bowl.

skirt \SKURT\ (v.) -ed, -ing
to evade; pass close by, circle around
For fun, Shanna sometimes asked her parents where babies came from just to watch them uncomfortably **skirt** the issue.

sluggish \SLUG ish\ (adj.)
lazy, inactive
After eating a huge turkey dinner, Timmy felt so **sluggish** that he took a nap.

smug \SMUG\ (adj.)
excessively self-satisfied
Shanna felt **smug** after she found out that Chantalle had paid twice as much as she had for the same pair of jeans.

sociable \SO shu bul\ (adj.)
friendly, gracious

Derek thinks it's easy to be **sociable** at the pool hall, because he can just walk up to a table and offer to split a game with someone.

solace \SOL is\ (n.)
comfort in distress; consolation

Ashley took **solace** in the fact that, even though it was raining that day, the sun would come out tomorrow.

solicitous \su LIS ih tus\ (adj.)
concerned, attentive; eager

Willow was extremely **solicitous** to the animals at the shelter, giving them food and water and much needed love.

solitary \SOL ih ter ee\ (adj.)
alone; remote, secluded

George felt as though he were in **solitary** confinement, but really, he was just the only kid in detention that day.

soluble \SOL yu bul\ (adj.)
capable of being solved or dissolved

Timmy licked his lips as he watched the **soluble** hot cocoa mix dissolve in his cup as he added hot water.

soothe \SOOTH\ (v.) -ed, -ing
to calm, placate; comfort
After a tough day of fighting for the environ-ment, Willow practiced yoga to **soothe** her nerves and bring her back to a "happy place."

specious \SPEE shus\ (adj.)
plausible but incorrect
Shanna understood that her "there's no such thing as global warming" position was **specious**, but she had to argue it fully if she wanted her team to win the debate.

spontaneous \spon TAY nee us\ (adj.)
on the spur of the moment, impulsive
In an effort to be more **spontaneous**, Paul suddenly serenaded Marisol in the middle of the lunchroom.

sprint \SPRINT\ (v.) -ed, -ing
dash, run quick for short distances
George **sprinted** across the schoolyard like lightning when he spotted his friend holding a bag of doughnuts on the other side.

sprout \SPROWT\ (v.) -ed, -ing
emerge and develop rapidly; to grow
Shanna thought her cousin had **sprouted** six inches since the last time she had seen her, but it turned out her cousin was just wearing platforms.

spurious \SPYOOR ee uss\ (adj.)
   lacking authenticity, false
   Someone started a **spurious** rumor that Timmy
   is going to be valedictorian, but there's no doubt
   that Shanna has the better grade point average.

squander
   \SKWAN der\ (v.) -ed, -ing
   to waste
   George's parents think he
   squanders away time
   perusing the Internet, but
   George counts it as a real
   learning experience.

squelch \SKWELCH\ (v.) -ed, -ing
   to suppress, to put down with force
   Derek **squelched** the drummer's idea that the
   band should change their name from Snakebite
   to Bite of the Viperpuss.

stagnant \STAG nent\ (adj.)
   immobile, stale
   George couldn't tell if the awful smell was
   coming from the **stagnant** water in the nearby
   puddle or his armpits.

statute \STA choot\ (n.)
   law, edict
   Willow was outraged when a new town **statute**
   stated that starting tomorrow all kids under
   eighteen would have a ten o'clock curfew.

stealthily \STELTH ih lee\ (adv.)
covertly, secretly
Paul **stealthily** approached Marisol's locker and slipped a rose inside it when she wasn't looking.

stern \STURN\ (adj.)
strict, harsh, severe
Josh knew his mom meant business when she gave him a **stern** look that told him to take his feet off the coffee table.

stifle \STY ful\ (v.) -ed, -ing
to smother or suffocate; suppress
Paul **stifled** a laugh when he saw the bald principal chasing his toupee in the wind across the school parking lot.

stimulate \STIM yu layt\ (v.) -ed, -ing
to excite, provoke
Timmy wrote three topics on a piece of paper, hoping one of them would **stimulate** an interesting conversation on his date.

stoic \STOH ik\ (adj.)
indifferent to or unaffected by emotions
Josh's expression was **stoic**, considering that he had just accidentally slammed his locker door on his finger.

stomp \STAHMP\ (v.) -ed, -ing
step heavily
Shanna **stomped** into her sister Lisa's room and accused Lisa of taking her strawberry lip gloss.

straddle \STRA del\ (v.) -ed, -ing
be on both sides of something
Willow finds it infuriating when politicians **straddle** issues rather than take stands.

stump \STUMP\ (v.) -ed, -ing
to challenge; to baffle
Timmy spent the entire day trying to solve the crossword puzzle, but he couldn't; he was totally **stumped**.

sturdy \STUR dee\ (adj.)
firm, well built, stout
Shanna prefers strappy sandals to the **sturdy** loafers that her mother wears.

submissive \sub MISS iv\ (adj.)
tending to meekness, to submit to the will of others
Josh was **submissive** when the officer pulled him over for speeding; he did exactly what he was told without argument.

subsist \sub SIST\ (v.) -ed, -ing
stay alive; survive
No matter how delicious chocolate bars are, one cannot **subsist** on chocolate alone.

substantiate \sub STAN she ayt\ (v.) -ed, -ing
to verify, confirm, provide supporting evidence
Timmy camped in his backyard with his telescope and his camera, determined to **substantiate** his theory that aliens really were hovering nearby.

subterfuge
\SUB ter fyooj\ (n.)
deceptive strategy
Ashley thought her date used **subterfuge** to get out of seeing her that weekend; he said he had to babysit his little brother, but Ashley knew he didn't have a little brother.

subvert \sub VURT\ (v.) -ed, -ing
to undermine or corrupt
Chantalle tried to **subvert** Shanna's diet by eating a hot fudge sundae in front of her and talking about how delicious it was.

succumb \su KUM\ (v.) -ed, -ing
to give in to a stronger power; yield
Shanna **succumbed** to her desire for hot fudge and ice cream and ordered a sundae.

suffice \suh FIYS\ (v.) -ed, -ing
meet requirements, be capable
Josh really wanted to date a girl named Belinda, but since Belinda didn't like him, Josh decided that her twin sister, Brenda, would **suffice**.

sully \SUL ee\ (v.) -ied, -ing
to soil, stain, tarnish, taint
Willow **sullied** her jeans with dirt while planting a tree in her backyard.

superficial \soo per FISH ul\ (adj.)
hasty; shallow and phony
Most people think Chantalle is **superficial** because all she cares about are clothes and parties.

superstitious \soo per STISH iss\ (adj.)
one irrationally believes that completely unrelated circumstances can influence an event
Willow is a little **superstitious**, but not enough to carry around a poor, innocent little bunny rabbit's foot for good luck.

supplant \suh PLANT\ (v.) -ed, -ing
to replace, substitute
Brenda dated Josh for two weeks before Belinda got jealous and **supplanted** her.

supple \SUPl\ (adj.)
flexible, pliant
Willow brushed the soft and **supple** leaf across her cheek . . . before she realized that it was poison ivy.

suppress \suh PRESS\ (v.) -ed, -ing
to end an activity or subdue
Derek could not **suppress** his smile when he saw the huge crowd who had come to hear his band.

surfeit \SIR fit\ (n.)
excessive amount
Timmy was bummed by the **surfeit** of spam in his e-mail and vowed to get a filtering program.

surplus \SIR plus\ (n.)
excess
The lunch lady slid the **surplus** mystery meat into the fridge after the lunch period was over.

surreptitious \sir up TISH iss\ (adj.)
secret, stealthy
Paul performed the card trick in homeroom so **surreptitiously** that nobody knew how he had done it.

surrogate \SIR uh git\ (n.)
a substitute; one filling in for someone else
Paul acted as a **surrogate** for his friend when he went onstage during open-mic night at the comedy club.

suspend \su SPEND\ (v.) -ed, -ing
to defer, interrupt; dangle, hang
Shanna **suspended** her extracurricular activities in order to study for finals.

swarm \SWARM\ (n.)
a large number of insects traveling in a group
Chantalle was inundated by a **swarm** of mosquitoes after spraying herself with a new perfume.

sycophant \SIK u fant\ (n.)
self-serving flatterer; yes-man

Marisol wanted to date a guy who had his own opinion on matters, not a **sycophant** who agreed with everything she said.

symmetry
\SIM eh tree\ (n.)
equality and balance in objects

For the school art show, Marisol hung an all-black canvas next to an all-white one and titled them "Perfect **Symmetry**."

synergy \sin er jee\ (n.)
cooperative interaction producing greater results

The coach complemented the team's amazing **synergy**, which is what led them to win the game.

synthesize \SIN thi siyz\ (v.) -ed, -ing
to produce artificially

Derek preferred going to a live rock concert, as opposed to listening to a **synthesized** imitation on a CD.

tact \TAKT\ (n.)
consideration in dealing with others, skill in not offending others
Shanna agreed that the outfit she tried on was not very flattering, but Chantalle could have commented with more **tact**, rather than pointing and laughing at it.

talisman \TAL iss man\ (n.)
magic object that offers supernatural protection
Ashley's mom hung a small **talisman** around the rearview mirror of the family car to protect them from accidents.

tangential \tan JEN shul\ (adj.)
digressing, diverting
The teacher told Josh that she'd answer his **tangential** question after class because she had a lot of information to cover and needed to stay on point.

tangible \TAN ji bul\ (adj.)
able to be sensed, perceptible, measurable
Shanna snapped a picture of Lisa reading Shanna's diary; now she had **tangible** evidence to show her parents.

taunt \TAWNT\ (v.) -ed, -ing
to ridicule, mock, insult
George **taunted** the monkeys at the zoo by shoving bananas in his mouth and scratching his sides while they were watching.

temerity
\te MEH ri tee\ (n.)
recklessness, fearlessness
George said that he had the **temerity** to go cliff diving, but nobody believed him.

temperance \TEM per unss\ (n.)
restraint, self-control, moderation
Marisol showed great **temperance** when she passed the table packed with delicious desserts and took only four.

tenable \TEHN uh buhl\ (adj.)
defensible, reasonable
The teacher thought that asking her students to read three books over spring break was a **tenable** request, but the students disagreed.

tenacious \ten AY shiss\ (adj.)
determined, keeping a firm grip on
The cheerleading squad practiced their routines **tenaciously** because they wanted to win the national competition.

tentative \TEN tu tiv\ (adj.)
not fully worked out; uncertain
Shanna made a **tentative** agreement to go out with her friends on Friday night, but had to check her calendar to confirm that she was free.

testimony \TESS ti moh nee\ (n.)
statement made under oath
George was glued to the television as he watched the witness's damning **testimony** on his favorite law show.

therapeutic \ther uh PYOO tik\ (adj.)
medicinal
Josh gulped down the nasty herbal drink, thinking it was **therapeutic**, but in reality it had no medicinal qualities at all.

thicket \THIK et\ (n.)
dense bushes
Paul watched the squirrels chase each other across the grass, then into a nearby **thicket**, out of sight.

throng \THRONG\ (n.)
a large group of people, crowd
Every Saturday a **throng** of kids gathered for a bonfire on the beach.

thwart \THWART\ (v.) -ed, -ing
to block or prevent from happening; frustrate
The rain **thwarted** Josh's plans for a romantic picnic, so he took his date to the movies instead.

timeless \TIYM les\ (adj.)
eternal, ageless
Although Marisol considers her bell-bottoms and cotton ponchos **timeless**, the rest of the school thinks that she sometimes looks like a throwback from the 1970s.

timorous \TIM uh rus\ (adj.)
timid, shy, full of apprehension
Ashley smiled at the **timorous** little girl who was hiding behind her mother on line at the drugstore.

toady \TOH dee\ (n.)
flatterer, hanger-on, yes-man
Chantalle likes to surround herself with **toadies** who hang on her every word and tell her she's awesome at least once a day.

tolerate \TOL uh rayt\ (v.) -ed, -ing
to endure, permit; to respect others
Shanna's little sister often drives her crazy, but Shanna **tolerates** it because she loves her.

tome \TOHM\ (n.)
book, usually large and academic
Timmy likes to browse through the **tomes** on aerospace engineering in his father's office.

torpid \TOR pid\ (adj.)
lethargic; unable to move; dormant
George was sleeping so **torpidly** that he didn't hear his alarm clock and was late for school.

touchstone \TUCH stohn\ (n.)
something used to test the excellence of others, standard
Ashley, who is warm, bright, and enthusiastic, is the **touchstone** for a happy student.

tractable \TRAK te bul\ (adj.)
easily managed or controlled, compliant
The teacher awarded the **tractable** class with a pizza party and a day of no homework.

transcribe \tran SKRIYB\ (v.) -ed, -ing
to copy, reproduce, record
Willow got a cramp in her hand as she **transcribed** every word the teacher said into her notebook.

transient \TRANZ ee ent\ (adj.)
temporary, short-lived, fleeting
Ashley's grumpy mood that morning was **transient**; by second period she was her usual cheery self.

travesty \TRA ves tee\ (n.)
parody, exaggerated imitation, caricature
Timmy thought getting detention for the one prank he played on the school bully was a **travesty** of justice.

tremulous \TREM yoo luss\ (adj.)
trembling; quivering; fearful, timid
Willow's **tremulous** puppy sat shivering under the dining room table as thunder and lightning cracked around the house.

trepidation \treh pih DAY shuhn\ (n.)
fear and anxiety
Timmy crept down the dark staircase into the school basement with **trepidation** because Paul was behind him making scary noises the whole way.

truculent \TRUHK yuh lent\ (adj.)
belligerent, disposed to fighting
Josh, the school bully, vowed to give up his **truculent** ways as soon as he graduated high school.

turpitude \TUR pi tood\ (n.)
inherent vileness, foulness, depravity
Timmy's mother said that television is to blame for most of the **turpitude** in society, and threw out the family's TV.

tutelage \TOOT uh lihj\ (n.) *guardianship, guidance*
Under Chantalle's patient **tutelage**, Ashley was able to learn the art of dancing in three-inch heels in time for the party.

tyro \TIE roh\ (n.)
beginner, novice
Timmy enjoyed teaching **tyros** the intricacies of chess.

ubiquitous

\yoo BIHK wih tis\ (adj.)
being everywhere
simultaneously
Fast food franchises are
ubiquitous in the United States.

unconscionable

\uhn KAHN shuhn uh buhl\ (adj.)
unscrupulous; shockingly unfair or unjust
Shanna thought it was **unconscionable** that
Chantalle would make a friendship bracelet for
Ashley and not for her.

unfrock \uhn FRAHK\ (v.) -ed, -ing

to dethrone, especially of priestly power
Timmy wished that someone would come along
and **unfrock** Josh as "King of the Jocks."

usury \YOO zhuh ree\ (n.)

the practice of lending money at exorbitant rates
Josh got in trouble with the coach for practicing
usury when he loaned a guy on the basketball
team twenty bucks at 100 percent interest.

variegated \VAAR ee uh gayt ehd\ (adj.)
varied; marked with different colors
Marisol surprised her parents for their anniversary when she repainted the old kitchen in **variegated** primary colors.

vehemently \VEE uh muhnt lee\ (adv.)
marked by extreme intensity of emotions or convictions
Willow was **vehemently** against going to the prom—not because she didn't believe in proms, but because she didn't have a date.

veracity \vuhr AA sih tee\ (n.)
accuracy; truth
The **veracity** of the statement "all guys are dogs" is highly debatable.

verbose \vuhr BOHS\ (adj.)
wordy
Shanna wondered if her two-hour valedictorian speech was going to be a bit **verbose**.

verisimilitude \vehr uh sih MIHL ih tood\ (n.)
quality of appearing true or real
The TV show's **verisimilitude** led viewers to believe that the characters it portrayed were real people.

veritable \VEHR iht uh buhl\ (adj.)
being without question, often used figuratively
Josh thought the all-girl's high school down the block was a **veritable** gold mine for dates.

vernacular \vuhr NAA kyoo luhr\ (n.)
everyday language used by ordinary people; specialized language of a profession
The chemistry teacher tried to reach her students by using their **vernacular**, but she wound up sounding silly instead.

vernal \VUHR nuhl\ (adj.)
related to spring; fresh
Glad that winter was finally over, Paul breathed in the **vernal** spring air as he walked along the tulip-lined path in the school's quad.

vicariously
\vie KAAR ee uhs lee\ (adv.)
felt or undergone as if one were taking part in the experience or feelings of another
Shanna was too chicken to go on the Ferris wheel at the amusement park so she lived **vicariously** through Chantalle, who rode it three times and then told Shanna all about it.

vilify \ VIH lih fie \ (v.) -ied, -ing
to slander, defame
Josh knew he was wrong for taking the car without permission, but his mother didn't have to **vilify** him in front of his friends, did she?

vim \ VIHM \ (n.)
vitality and energy
Ashley's motto is: If you can't do it with **vim** and vigor, then don't do it at all.

vindicate \ VIHN dih kayt \ (v.) -ed, -ing
to clear of blame; support a claim
Josh blamed Paul for taking his baseball cards until Paul was **vindicated** when Josh found them buried at the bottom of his backpack.

virulent \ VEER yuh luhnt \ (adj.)
extremely poisonous; malignant; hateful
Derek could not go to the concert on Saturday because he had a **virulent** fever.

visceral \ VIHS uhr uhl \ (adj.)
instinctive, not intellectual; deep, emotional
Derek had a **visceral** reaction to the tune that his band keyboardist was playing and instinctively developed lyrics for it.

vituperate \ vih TOO puhr ayt \ (v.) -ed, -ing
to abuse verbally, berate
The principal fired the teacher when he heard her **vituperate** a student in class.

vociferous \voh sih fuhr uhs\ (adj.)
  loud, noisy
  Derek's mom told him to turn down his
  vociferous music.

volley \VAH lee\ (n.)
  a flight of missiles; round of gunshots
  Willow flinched when she thought she heard a
  volley of gunshots, but thankfully they were
  only firecrackers.

voluble \VAHL yuh buhl\ (adj.)
  *talkative, speaking
  easily, glib*
  Chantalle was forced
  to sit next to Timmy at
  the senior brunch and
  was surprised to find
  him fun and **voluble**.

W Y & Z

wan \WAHN\ (adj.)
sickly pale
Ashley's rosy complexion became **wan** when she spotted the thin envelope from her first-choice college in the mailbox. She had a feeling that it wasn't good news.

wanton \WAHN tuhn\ (adj.)
undisciplined, unrestrained; reckless
Derek's **wanton** image of a rocker is not a very good gauge of his personality.

wax \WAAKS\ (v.) -ed, -ing
to increase gradually; to begin to be
Ashley didn't start high school as the best student, but she has **waxed** her dedication to studying every year.

wield \WEELD\ (v.) -ed, -ing
to exercise authority or influence effectively
Timmy **wielded** the power of his extensive vocabulary by writing an essay that his English teacher needed a dictionary to read.